Wordsworth Donisthorpe

**Principles of Plutology**

Wordsworth Donisthorpe

**Principles of Plutology**

ISBN/EAN: 9783743330481

Manufactured in Europe, USA, Canada, Australia, Japa

Cover: Foto ©ninafisch / pixelio.de

Manufactured and distributed by brebook publishing software (www.brebook.com)

Wordsworth Donisthorpe

**Principles of Plutology**

# PRINCIPLES OF PLUTOLOGY.

BY

WORDSWORTH DONISTHORPE.

WILLIAMS AND NORGATE,
14, HENRIETTA STREET, COVENT GARDEN, LONDON;
AND 20, SOUTH FREDERICK STREET, EDINBURGH.
1876.

## ERRATUM.

Page 34, line 2, for "*Teological*," read "Teleological."

# CONTENTS.

## INTRODUCTION.

PAGE

Signs of the Times—The name "Political Economy"—Objections to name "Plutology"—Aim of Present Work—Differences between Political Economy and Plutology—Practical and Speculative Sciences—Technical Terms—Wage-fund and Wages disappear—De Quincey on the Object of Political Economy—Arrangement of the following Chapters . . . . . . 1—7

## CHAPTER I.
### ON THE FAILURES OF POLITICAL ECONOMY.

Science of Wealth Desirable—Is Political Economy that Science?—Glance at its History—Adam Smith, Ricardo, McCulloch, Mill, Bastiat, Cairnes—Reflected Lustre of Free-Trade—Cairnes' Attempt to Revive Economical Science—Succeeding Scepticism—Hearn—Time Arrived for True Science of Plutology—Anarchy in Domain of Political Economy: 1st, As to its Nature and Object; is it Practical or Speculative? Art or Science? 2nd, As to its Method, Inductive or Deductive? Qualitative or Quantitative? Exact or Hypothetical? 3rd, As to its Definitions, Wealth, Productive Labour, Capital, Value—Classification—Triumphs of Political Economy—Claims of Deductive School to—1st, Adam Smith's "Division of Labour;" 2nd, Adam Smith's "Free-Trade;" 3rd, Malthus' "Law of Population;" 4th, Ricardo's "Theory of Rent"—Fundamental Psychological Principles!—Positive Truths Discovered by Economists—Unobserved Growth of Plutology—Parallel Instances—Summary of Charges against Political Economy—Hostility of Working Classes Justified . . 9—36

## CHAPTER II.

#### CHARACTER AND OBJECTS OF PLUTOLOGY.

Its Position to be Defined—Origin of Vegetation and Soil—Analogous Origin of Mankind and Wealth — Mutual Adaptation — Definition of Wealth — Plutological Signification of "Useful"—Wealth not Necessarily Valuable—Wealth Measurable in Respect of Two Attributes—Difficulty of Measurement in Both Cases—Compound Ratios ready to Hand: Values—All Wealth Material and not Metaphysical—Position of Plutology in Classification of the Sciences—Relation between Plutology and Sociology Proper—Utility of this Branch of Study . . 37—51

## CHAPTER III.

#### METHOD OF PLUTOLOGY.

Premature-deductive Stage of a Science—Invention of General Laws—Induction must precede Deduction—Dr. Whewell on Stationary Periods—Aristotle and Ricardo — Inter-dependence of Values—Chemical Analogies: Analysis—Differences between Chemical and Plutological Methods—Spencer on the Conditions of Quantitative Science—Steps in Plutology: Colligation, Analysis, Generalisation, Classification, Deduction, and Prediction—Plutology no more Hypothetical than Astronomy, but more affected by Disturbing Causes—Errors lead to Corrected Theory 52—60

## CHAPTER IV.

#### DATA OF PLUTOLOGY.

Necessity for Accepting Data from Other Sciences—Degrees of Want—Degrees of Utility—Degrees of Limitation or Abundance—Institution of Property or Ownership—Exchange—Competition and Value—Price—Rise of General Values Absurd, of Prices Possible and Actual—Value not the Measure of Wealth—Unequal Distribution of Wealth—Curves of Wealth in Different Countries . . . . . . . . 61—71

## CHAPTER V.

#### COMBINATION.

Directly-gratificable and Indirectly-gratificable—Degrees of Indirectness—Consumption, Essential and

CONTENTS. vii

PAGE

Accidental—Fixed and Circulating Capital: Mill —Tools and Materials—Engines, Horses, Men, as Tools—Groundless Distinction in Treating of them—Wages—Adam Smith and McCulloch on Man—Analysis of Engine and of Man—Important Element Omitted by all Economists—Man as Proprietor and as Labourer—Importance of Keeping them Apart—Property in Man's Own Body—Values of Horses and Men—On Property and its Meanings . . . . . . 72—86

## CHAPTER VI.
### ANALYSIS.

Imperfect Analysis—Proximate and Ultimate Analysis — Economists Adopt a Middle Course — Remarkable Results—Quantitative Analysis—Analysis of Brick-wall as an Example—Illustration: Analysis of a Suit of Clothes—The Tailor and Cloth-merchant—The Weaver, Spinner, and Comber—Subsidiary Processes—The Combing Shed—Outlay and Cost of Working—Rent of Land, Buildings, and Shafting—Machinery, Coals, Oil, Soap, and Sundries—The Various Kinds of Labourers—The Comber's Profits—More Complete Analysis of the Labourers and of the Machinery—The Wool-broker and Sheep-farmer — Successive Facilities of Analyses—Table showing the Steps of the Process from the Sheep's Back to Our Own—Desideratum: a Book of Analyses—Analyses More or Less Complete . . . . . . 87—106

## CHAPTER VII.
### ON SOME PROMINENT ELEMENTS.

Labourers—Commodities with Large and Small Proportions of Labourers—Varieties of Labourers: their Values—The Combiner—Elements of Transport—Soil and Land—Land an Element of Cost of Production—Buckle, Fawcett, and Mill on the Point—Analogous Instances—Effects of Decline in Value of Park-lands . . . 107—118

## CHAPTER VIII.
### SYNTHESIS.

The Cause of Procrastinated Consumption—The "Wages of Abstinence" a Mere Fiction — Saving not Rewarded—Fructifying Causes—In-

terest or Average Profits—Value of Combiners—
Rise and Fall—Credit Panics—Manufacturers'
Notions of Profits . . . . . . 119—128

## CHAPTER IX.

### THE LAWS OF VALUE.

Nomenclature: Elements, Compounds, Co-elements, Substitutes — Enumeration not Analysis — Mill on Effectual Demand and Supply—Sellers and Buyers—Resolution of his Equation into Three Simple Laws—The term "Demand" dispensed with except in the Sense of "Desire"—How the Values of Things are Determined—Illustration: Imaginary Auction—Market-value and Permanent-value of Mill—Origin of Latter Notion—Rhythmical Fluctuations in Values—Mill's Three Kinds of Difficulty of Attainment—Cost of Production—Real Causes of Lowered Cost of Production—Two Forces at Work—Exceptions to so-called Law of Cost—True Laws of Value—Fashions: Tendency of Stimulated Desire—First Law of Value—Second Law—Third Law—Fourth Law—Illustrations—Wool and Cotton—Labourers and Machinery—Other General Laws Discoverable only by Induction . . . . . 129—159

## CHAPTER X.

### CLASSIFICATION.

Analysis must Precede Classification—Some Crude Attempts—Objections—Recent False Views on Classification Generally—Appropriate Basis of Classification is not the Genealogical one in Plutology as in the Animal and Vegetable Kingdoms—True Basis, Conformity to Same Laws of Variation . . . . . . . 160—169

ESSAY ON CAPITAL . . . . 171—185

# INTRODUCTION.

THE last decade has witnessed ominous symptoms of disease in the politico-economical system, violent convulsions, complete incapacity for assimilation, and consequent stoppage of growth. To drop the metaphor, the most unbridled scepticism has manifested itself with respect to all, or nearly all, the recognised doctrines of the established school, and the barrenness of the latter as regards results serves fully to justify the contempt into which it has fallen. In short, the study of wealth has been passing through a transitional period as thorough as that through which alchemy passed on its way to chemistry.

The time has now arrived for the butterfly to make its way out of the chrysalis, and the present short treatise is a well-meant, if feeble, attempt to extricate it from the tangled web of its own creation.

From the publication of the *Wealth of Nations* downwards treatises on the subject have appeared under the title, with but few exceptions, of *Political Economy*. The name of *Plutology* has been adopted by two or three writers, but, as a rule, has been discountenanced, probably from a general feeling that there was something radically different between political economy and the other sciences, which precluded the use of a title formed on the same model.

This objection does not hold with respect to the science of wealth as treated in this work, and the more technical designation has, therefore, been retained. From this it will be clear that it is intended to set the subject upon a new and perfectly scientific basis—in fact, to create a science out of what has hitherto been an undigested heap of observed facts. The title and rank of an exact science is claimed for Plutology. It stands on as firm a footing as Chemistry. It *is* what many have supposed Political Economy to be, the Science of Wealth.

Some of the salient points of difference between the science and its predecessor may now be anticipated. In the first place, whereas the latter was almost invariably treated as a practical science, or, what comes to the same thing, as an art aiming at the solution of definite problems; plutology, on the other hand, is a purely speculative science, dealing solely with the relations subsisting between phenomena.

"The object of political economy," says McCulloch, "is to point out the means by which the industry of man may be rendered most productive of those necessaries, comforts, and enjoyments which constitute wealth; to ascertain the circumstances most favourable for its accumulation; the proportions in which it is divided among the different classes of the community; and the mode in which it may be most advantageously consumed."

There is no doubt that this is what has been commonly understood to be the object of political economy by all writers on the subject (Professor Cairnes, perhaps, excepted), and it is herein that plutology differs from it; caring nothing for the practical rules which may be deduced from its doctrines, or for the circumstances favourable or unfavourable to the accumulation of wealth; less still for the mode in which it is distributed amongst its proprietors. All these questions it leaves to the practical politician, or moralist, or man of business. Plutology investigates the laws of value. That is all. In other words, it points out the relations which subsist between the values of things, and the uniformity or invariability of those relations.

For instance: coals are dearer in England just now. Plutology asks, What will be the effect on the value of labourers? Will wages rise or fall, and how much? Not, What must we do to keep coals down, or to prevent labourers from suffering thereby? or any like practical question.

At the same time we must not lose sight of an important fact which seems to have escaped the notice of Mr. H. Sidgwick in the introduction to his *Methods of Ethics*. It is this. That the same method which will enable us to predict an unseen effect from a known cause will also enable us to perform the inverse operation of following up a given effect to its unknown cause or causes. For example: given the present positions and motions of the planets, and the astronomer can predict the position they will respectively occupy ten years hence. So, given the position they will occupy in ten years, and he can tell us what position they occupy now. And by a little extension of his reasoning from a hypothetical or imaginary position he can predict the positions the planets would occupy in a given time; or, *vice versâ*, from the same data ascertain what would have been the positions a given number of years previously. In short, from a real or hypothetical given effect, speculative science can reason back to a certain, or probable, or possible cause, according to the nature and perfection of the science. The practical sciences profess from a given desirable end to discover the means to its attainment, and this is nothing more than one of the problems of the speculative sciences; so that, in point of fact, a practical science is but the application of the homologous speculative science to the solution of a problem of a particular description.

Of course a vague, meaningless question can receive no solution. "*Prudens interrogatio dimidium scientiæ.*" The plutologist is as unable to answer the questions stated by McCulloch as the geometer would be to declare which is the best form of trapezium, or as the chemist to point out what proportions of the elements conduce most to the welfare of the human organism. If the plutologist be asked whether a high ratio of valueless to valuable wealth is preceded by a high or low ratio of the value of labourers to that of machinery, an answer is possible.

Plutology and political economy differ secondly in respect of definitions.

The invariably-consistent application of technical terms is probably more uncommon in treatises on political economy than on any other scientific subject; and the reason is that most of those terms are in everyday use, and, like most homely expressions, they are indifferently employed to convey any one of several meanings. For example, the word "valuable," as has frequently been pointed out, is used to denote things supposed by the speaker to be highly useful or beneficial, whether exchangeable for much or little of other commodities. An old man in a cottage is praised for regarding his Bible as more valuable than all his furniture, whereas the former is worth ninepence and the latter ten pounds.

"Capital," again, is a much-abused term in trade, and still more so is "circulating capital," which is employed by business men to denote a money-fund for the payment of current expenses, including wages. "Wealth" in some works on political economy means anything that affords satisfaction to man, whether of value or not, such as air, water, food, dress, pictures; in others it means only such things as have an exchangeable value, which air has not. And even the adopters of the more restricted acceptation split upon another rock, the one part including slaves, the other rejecting humanity as that for which wealth exists, and therefore not itself wealth. "Labour," "production," "profits," "interest," "demand," "supply," &c., &c., are equally ill-defined.

All these and many other similarly situated terms will receive a careful definition in the course of this work.

Probably one of the most remarkable features in the new system will at first appear to be the total rejection of the theories of wages and the wage-fund, heretofore regarded as fundamental and demonstrable. Wages will be regarded throughout as simply the price of one of the important elements in the composition of most products, and as such it will require no distinctive appellation any more than the price paid for the use of machinery or horses.

The supposed reciprocal relations of wages and profits are soon seen to dissolve in face of the chemical method of plutology. And many other world-renowned and venerable doctrines fall simultaneously.

"What is the ground of exchangeable value? My hat, for example, bears the same value as your umbrella, double the value of my shoes, four times the value of my gloves, one-twentieth of the value of this watch. Of these several relations of value what is the sufficient cause?" (*De Quincey*, 1862, vol. iv., p. 189.)

Such is the question in De Quincey's own words, which it was the business of political economy to answer, and up to the present day it has remained unanswered. It remains to be seen whether the question really is unanswerable, or whether plutology can obtain a solution where political economy has so signally failed.

I need not further anticipate the arguments contained in succeeding chapters of this volume. Enough has already been said or hinted to insure its being instantly relegated to the flames, or the library whence it came, by all orthodox and confirmed political economists. Fortunately, however, there is an outside public, a very large proportion of whom are engaged in the production of wealth, and to whom a sincere attempt at placing the objects of their daily study on a truly philosophical foundation will be welcome.

The first chapter consists entirely of a criticism of political economy as it is. The second and third chapters investigate the nature and method of a true science of wealth. The data of plutology are then treated of. But Chapters V. and VI., on Combination and Analysis, form the keystone of the work. In Chapter VII. certain prominent elements—namely, labourers, transport elements, and land — receive a separate consideration; and Chapter VIII. is occupied with combination from the synthetical standpoint, and the subject of profits is reviewed and the true nature of interest explained. The laws of value are enunciated in the ninth chapter, and the tenth and last treats of plutological classification and definitions, and is followed by an essay on "The Definition of Capital." The essay was written in 1874, and forms the nucleus of the present volume.

# PRINCIPLES OF PLUTOLOGY.

## CHAPTER I.

### POLITICAL ECONOMY.

GRANTED that if no science of wealth yet exists, it is high time that it should; still the question remains whether political economy is that science. Fairly to answer this question, it will be well to glance over the whole history of this branch of study, in order to avoid the charge of first misrepresenting the subject and then approving or condemning it accordingly.

Passing over such scintillations of genius as Locke's remarks on labour and riches and Voltaire's hints of free trade; over the anticipation of economic truths by the pamphleteers of the seventeenth and eighteenth centuries; over the wild so-called physiocratic system which appeared satisfactory to Quesnay and Turgot, we come to the foundation and establishment of political economy, to all intents and purposes as it exists at the present day, by Adam Smith.

Is it necessary to qualify this last statement by the admission that considerable development has of course taken place in the hands of such thinkers as Malthus,

Ricardo, Say, McCulloch, Mill, Bastiat, Cairnes, and Hearn? To deny this would be one thing; it is quite another thing to assert that no such change has been effected in the method or principles of the subject as would justify us in affirming that a new science has sprung up on the ruins of an old one, as astronomy supplanted astrology, or as alchemy made way for chemistry. Indeed, it is remarkable how little the student of the *Wealth of Nations* has to learn or unlearn in his passage thence to modern economical treatises. We are justified, it may be repeated, in considering political economy, from Smith downwards, as a whole; and the various dissentients on particular points rather as sects of the one faith than as Turks, infidels, and heretics.

After premising this a stronger light may with advantage be thrown upon the said differences and disputes. Adam Smith had, in all probability, no idea that the terms borrowed from trade by which he was wont to explain his meaning would be treated by his successors as technical expressions, and as such, loose and vague as they were, cramped within the compass of rigidly-scientific definitions and then subjected to the most searching analysis. Not one of Smith's terms could aspire to even tolerable precision; and it is to Ricardo that we are indebted for the application of the strict geometrical method to the phenomena of wealth. Such treatment, it is needless to observe, required the most rigid adherence to exact definition.

These restrictions and limitations soon became intolerable, and one by one succeeding writers broke loose, and, as in all reactions against tyranny, ran riot with the most audacious disregard of the great dogmatist's formulas. J. B. Say quarrels with his definition of value, and, later on, McCulloch proclaims the most startling heresy with respect to capital, appealing in corroboration thereof to the high authority of Adam Smith. But, in spite of these renewed and increasing attacks, the Ricardian system maintains its position, and by means of its terms and methods, theorems are demonstrated and further conclusions based thereon with a mathematical accuracy previously undreamed of. And whatever doubts as to its future fate may have subsequently prevailed, they were quickly dispelled—at least for a long season—by the appearance on the scene of John Stuart Mill's world-famous work. Nor did the ingenuity of a Bastiat, armed though it was with the higher political philosophy, avail to overturn the newly-supported edifice. The success of the practical systems based upon the reasonings of economical writers, particularly of the doctrine of free trade, served to reflect considerable glory upon the somewhat mysterious source, and hence it befell that the science was in danger of being choked by its own offspring. Economists busied themselves in political agitations with which they had no concern, neglecting the pure and unexciting investigations of theory for the dazzling attractions of the art of government. The late Professor Cairnes was the first to point this out, and to bring back, or rather try to bring back, the truant *savants* to their duties. The result of this partly-effectual attempt has been to bring the whole subject once more under the consideration of unprejudiced minds, and to display in all their nakedness the glaring inconsistencies and discrepancies which disgrace it. It has become clear that all, or very nearly all, the old definitions are vague or impracticable, that old landmarks must be swept away, and that the whole field must be re-surveyed by free and untrammelled inquirers. Hearn's *Plutology*, based as it is on this assumption, without, however, swerving from the accepted method of political economy, reminds us in its freshness, its freedom of scope, and its vigorous and independent style, of the only economical treatise which deserves comparison with it — the *Wealth of Nations*. Of other recent publications it is needless to say more than that they are all imbued with the spirit of scepticism and rebellion against authority, without giving promise of substituting anything better that is new in the place of the rejected old.

Whether the present work fulfils this requirement it is for the public to decide. Such, indeed, is its object. This first chapter is simply an attempt to demonstrate the futility and barrenness of political economy in its very essence; and the remainder of the work will be devoted to the establishment, on a philosophic basis, of a true science of plutology.

In every branch of inquiry there are certain fundamental points upon which all parties must be agreed before a science can be said to exist. For instance, all zoologists are agreed that the structure of plants forms no part of their province. Botanists, again, would all concur in rejecting such a definition of their science as the following:—" The object of botany is to point out the means by which the vegetable world may be rendered most productive of food, medicines, and other requirements of life; to ascertain the circumstances most favourable to their accumulation; and the mode in which they may be most advantageously consumed." Geometricians, again, are agreed that the inductive process is inapplicable to the subject of their investigation. Should a contributor to some mathematical journal inform the public that after the most careful and laborious measurement and comparison of no fewer than 10,000 plates, quoits, balls, hoops, and other circular objects, he had ascertained that the circumference of a circle was exactly $3\frac{1}{7}$th of the diameter, would not the results of his induction be laughed to scorn?

And now what is the position of political economy in this respect? Verbatim extracts from admitted authorities are necessary in order to expose the true state of affairs; but they shall be cut as short as is compatible with explicitness.

And, first, is political economy a speculative or a practical science? In other words, is it a science or an art? McCulloch thus describes it:—" The object of political economy is to point out the means by which the industry of men may be rendered most productive of all those necessary comforts and enjoyments which constitute wealth; to ascertain the circumstances most favourable for its accumulation; the proportions in which it is divided among the different classes of the community, and the mode in which it may be most advantageously consumed." Is this description a fair one? If so, political economy is, after all, not a science but an art; it is defined by its end, and consists, not of laws, but of rules. It falls into one category together with navigation, ethics, legislation, engineering, &c., as opposed to astronomy, morality, jurisprudence, mechanics, &c., which, unconcerned with practice, merely investigate the uniform relations subsisting between phenomena.

Surely, O political economists! here is a question sufficiently fundamental:—What are you trying to do? What is your object? You must be unanimous at least in this. And so Professor Hearn would have us believe. "Political economy, indeed, has rarely, except in name, been ever regarded as a science. It is as an art that the older economists have always treated it; it is as an art that Adam Smith defines the term; it is as an art that it has acquired its present popularity; it is as an art that even those who insist upon its scientific rank habitually discuss it. . . . . . Mr. J. S. Mill avowedly follows the example of Smith." In spite of all this Professor Hearn himself proposes to write a strictly scientific treatise on the subject of wealth, entitled *Plutology*, and yet, to use his own words, certain desires and "efforts, and the contrivances by which either their result is increased or their amount diminished, and the circumstances favourable or unfavourable to such contrivances, form the subject of this inquiry."

Whether the true science of wealth is eventually

treated of in the *Plutology* may, then, be guessed, by those who have not seen it, from the description of its subject thus given by the author himself.

Meanwhile, *Audi alteram partem*. Professor Cairnes, in his clear and able vindication of the scientific claims of political economy, thus argues:—" But, secondly, the ordinary definition represents political economy as a science, and (as I have elsewhere said) for those who clearly apprehend what 'science,' in the modern sense of the term, means, this ought sufficiently at once to indicate its province and what it undertakes to do. Unfortunately many who perfectly understand what 'science' means when the word is employed with reference to physical nature, allow themselves to slide into a totally different sense of it, or rather into acquiescence in an absence of all distinct meaning in its use, when they employ it with reference to social existence. In the minds of a large number of people everything is social science which proposes to deal with social facts, either in the way of remedying a grievance or in promoting order and progress in society. Everything is political economy which is in any way connected with the production, distribution, or consumption of wealth. Now I am anxious here to insist upon this fundamental point. Whatever takes the form of a plan aiming at definite practical ends—it may be a measure for the diminution of pauperism, for the reform of land tenure, for the extension of co-operative industry, for the regulation of the currency; or it may assume a more ambitious shape, and aim at reorganising society under spiritual and temporal powers represented by a high priest of humanity and three bankers—it matters not what the proposal be, whether wide or narrow in its scope, severely judicious or wildly imprudent—if its object be to accomplish definite practical ends, then I say it has none of the characteristics of a science, and has no just claim to the name." Whereupon proof follows that political economy is, after all, a science in the fullest acceptation of the term, and that all matter contained in treatises on that subject devoted to the consideration of definite practical ends is irrelevant, wide of the mark, and merely the result of corrupt practices which have gradually crept into the economical department of scientific inquiry.

It is no part of my purpose in this place to inquire which of these two diametrically opposite opinions on a fundamental point, each stoutly advocated by acknowledged champions, is the true one. Discord exists; that is demonstrated; and I shall now proceed to show how upon another almost equally vital question the most complete anarchy prevails.

Next to the object of a particular branch of inquiry nothing is so important, so fundamental, as its method. Hear Professor Cairnes on this question:—

"This, then, being the character of political economy, we have to consider by what means the end which it proposes—the discovery of the laws of the production and distribution of wealth—may be most effectually promoted. To the question here indicated the answer most commonly given by those who take an interest in economic speculation is, 'By the inductive method of inquiry . . . . . . by induction (in the narrower sense as distinguished from deduction) in combination with observation and experiment. . . . . . . . Now to perceive the utter futility, the necessary impotence of such a method of proceeding as a means of solving economic problems, one has only to consider what the nature of those problems is." Mill holds the same opinion—pronounces the inverse concrete deductive method the most suitable for economical research. The same method is advocated by Professor Jevons under the title of "The Complete Method."

There are not wanting supporters of an opposite doctrine, and though their names do not carry so much weight singly, they are every day becoming more and more numerous; and the greater importance is to be attached to their remarks partly on this account and partly because it is becoming evident and generally admitted that all concrete sciences must first pass through an inductive before entering upon a deductive stage. Sciences not long since treated entirely on the deductive method have lately been brought into the arena of induction: witness Law, Morality, Jurisprudence, and Sociology. In Mr. McLeod's *Theory and Practice of Banking* we find the following :—" These principles, then, act with unerring certainty—they are universally true; human instinct is as certain, invariable, and universal in its nature as the laws of motion, and that is the circumstance which raises monetary science to the rank of an exact or inductive science." Passing over Professor Cairnes's very just criticism on the language of this proposition, it is clear the author intends to convey the notion that the inductive is the true method of political economy; and in this opinion he has the support of an increasing number of statisticians in this country, in France, and in America.

Then upon the question as to whether it is a mathematical science there are differences, and not all those who admit that it is so, also admit that it is an exact science. "To me it seems," writes Professor Jevons, "that our science must be mathematical simply because it deals with quantities." To which Professor Cairnes replies—"If I do not mistake, something more than this is needed to sustain Mr. Jevons's position."

And now comes the consideration of a third condition absolutely indispensable to scientific progress—unanimity with respect to the meanings to be attached to the technical terms employed.

To what extent does this prevail?

Short as it is, it is hardly worth while to go through the whole list of technical expressions employed in all treatises on this subject. Three or four of the most general and important will suffice to illustrate the confusion which exists. It is no part of the purpose of this chapter to point out which (if any) of the competitors is the true definition, or, in case all are unsatisfactory, to suggest a new one.

Wealth, at all events, being the subject with which the so-called science is concerned, ought surely to be clearly defined. Here is Mill's definition:—

"Wealth, then, may be defined as useful or agreeable things which possess exchangeable value; or, in other words, all useful or agreeable things except those which can be obtained in the quantity desired without labour or sacrifice." This is J. B. Say's interpretation, while Ricardo, on the other hand, renders the term co-extensive with commodities which are useful to us whether possessing exchangeable value or not.

According to this view, air, water, gold, and diamonds are all classed as wealth. Bastiat, in common, as he admits, with the vulgar, takes up a position midway between these two :—" Sometimes we hear them say the abundance of water is wealth to such a country. In this case they are thinking only of utility, but when one wishes to reckon up his own wealth he makes what is called an 'inventory,' in which only commercial value is taken into account. With deference to the *savants*, I believe that the vulgar are right for once. Wealth is either actual or relative. In the first point of view we judge of it by our satisfactions. Mankind become richer in proportion as they acquire a greater amount of ease or material prosperity, whatever be the commodities by which it is procured. But do you wish to know what proportional share each man has in the general prosperity—in other words, his relative wealth? This is simply a relation which value alone reveals, because value is itself a relation." There is much that is reasonable to be urged on either side; but M. Bastiat, stuffing his ears with wax, glides between Scylla and Charybdis with the utmost indifference.

So much for wealth. And next let us inquire what is productive labour? All labour is said to be either productive or unproductive, and the question arises, how are we to distinguish the one from the other? Mr. Scrope's readable little volume on political economy contains the following note:—"The difficulties with which the ultra-refining and mathematical school of economists have to contend are well exhibited in the disputes between them as to the limits of productiveness. Mr. Malthus (followed in this by Mr. J. S. Mill) denies that the labour of a cook, a coachman, an author or an actor is productive, though asserting the productiveness of that of a butcher, a coachmaker, a printer, and a scene-painter. Mr. McCulloch, running into the other extreme, insists that the occupations of billiard-playing, blowing soap-bubbles—nay, of eating, drinking, and sleeping—are productive." "I shall therefore," writes Mill, "in this treatise, when speaking of wealth, understand by it only what is called material wealth, and by productive labour only those kinds of exertion which produce utilities embodied in material objects. But in limiting myself to this sense of the word I mean to avail myself of the full extent of that restricted acceptation, and I shall not refuse the appellation productive to labour which yields no material product as its direct result, provided that an increase of material products is its ultimate consequence."

Without here mentioning a still further qualification which Mill afterwards imposes on the above, sufficient evidence has already been adduced to show that in this, as in previous instances, there is nothing like agreement to be found amongst political economists.

It may be said that, though these terms are doubtless important from a philosophical point of view, in practice they are not of much consequence. Such is Mr. Scrope's opinion. One more example shall therefore be selected, the practical importance of which no one can dispute. What is capital?

Inasmuch as a whole chapter is to be devoted to this question further on, let us here restrict ourselves to the much narrower question, Are land and labourers rightly classed under the head of capital? To this question four answers are logically conceivable, and only four:—Land, but not labourers; labourers, but not land; neither one nor the other; and lastly, both.

Is it credible that leading writers can be cited who among them return all four of these answers?

Such is the deplorable state of anarchy reigning in this department of inquiry that there is no difficulty in doing this. Mr. Macdonnel accepts land, but not labourers; Adam Smith, labourers, but not land; McCulloch accepts both; and Mill neither.

Probably value is the only technical term uniformly employed in the same sense by economists in general, and yet of this term Professor Jevons writes as follows:—" I have pointed out the excessive ambiguity of the word value, and the apparent impossibility of safely using it. Nothing more need be said at present on the subject of definitions, unless it be to recall the warning of Plato, quoted in

Mr. McLeod's work on banking:—'Know well, then, that worthy and godlike is the zeal with which you rush upon definitions. Apply yourself to it, and practise it while yet you are a novice—all the more because it seems useless, and is called trifling by the vulgar; for if you do not the truth will escape you.'"

Quitting altogether the subject of internal dissension, let us now turn our attention to the classification of the innumerable kinds of wealth. Search the libraries. Here is a table of the classification of plants. The whole vegetable kingdom is first split up into two sub-kingdoms—Phanerogamia and Cryptogamia. The former is split into two divisions—Angiospermia and Gymnospermia. Then Angiospermia consist of two classes—Dicotyledons and Monocotyledons. The Dicotyledons are divided into four sub-classes—Thalamifloræ, Calycifloræ, Corollifloræ, and Monochlamydeæ. Each of these sub-classes is subdivided into groups, the groups into orders, the orders into genera, the genera into species, and the species into varieties.

Again, consider the following arrangement of the Animal Kingdom:—

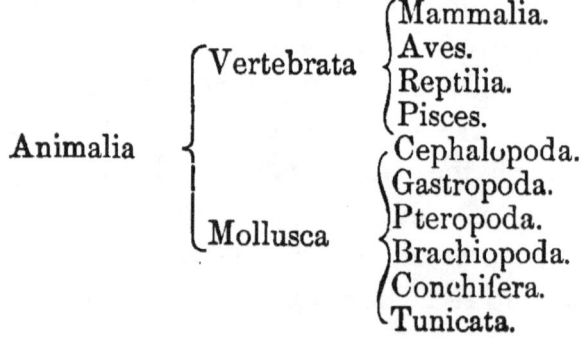

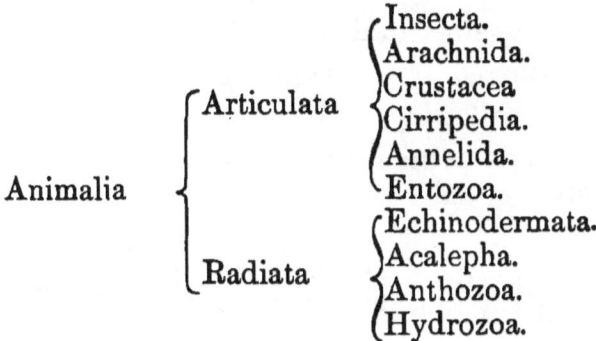

And then bear in mind that one alone of this list is the formidable Mammalia, with its almost countless genera, species, and varieties.

And what, now, has political economy to show? Where is Ricardo's system? Where is Mill's system? Compare them with Jussieu's and Endlicher's. First of all, where are they? "But," protest the supporters of political economy, "wealth does not naturally split up into families and groups genealogically related; the varieties of wealth have not all sprung from a common stock." Very good; then I appeal to mineralogy. Have we not sulphur, selenium, diamond, and graphite grouped together under the title of metalloids; then bismuth, arsenic, osmiridium, amalgam, iron, native copper, &c., under metals; and then the tellurides, and then the antimonides, the hydrous silicates, the borates, and so on to the end of the chapter? How is it, then, that not so much as a single table of classification is to be found throughout the whole field of economic literature? The answer is plain. Because no classification worthy of the title exists. The method employed is incompetent to produce it. True, a meagre, miserable, and altogether ludicrous table may be put together, as gathered from leading authorities. Such a table is the following, and it serves to exhibit in a focus the exact position of the science (?) with respect to classification :—

Wealth. {Valuable. / Not valuable.  {Productive. / Unproductive.  {Land. / Labour / Capital  {Fixed. / Circulating.

O shades of Linnæus, of Jussieu, of Cuvier, of Lindley, look down on this!

This is all we are told of the classification of such things as gold, wheat, cattle, water, tinkers, ploughs, actresses, beef, lace, barristers, cloth, coals, &c., &c. And even this is disputed, altered, wrangled over and torn to pieces by every new economist that enters the arena.

Great works have sometimes been accomplished with poor instruments; and it is contended by some who admit the deplorable condition of economical theory, that, nevertheless, great results have been attained by means of it. Indeed, great part of some treatises on the subject is taken up with crowing over the glories of free trade and the collapse of the mercantile system. It behoves us, therefore, to inquire fairly what these vaunted results are, and whether they are really to be attributed to the causes assigned to them. A challenge has indeed been thrown out to the advocates of a mathematical political economy to try their strength against the old school by a comparison of results. "If my view be unsound," writes Professor Cairnes, "there is at hand an easy means of refutation—the production of an economic truth, not before known, which has been thus arrived at. But I am not aware that up to the present any such evidence has been furnished of the efficacy of the mathematical method."

What, now, are these triumphs of scientific discovery so confidently appealed to?

First and foremost, in every sense of the words, comes the theory of the division of labour. No one will deny the paramount importance of Adam Smith's great discovery. Not only was it a grand generalisation, but it was followed, or rather accompanied, by a grand application. The mere fact that Smith first made a discovery and then struck out a method or founded a school of political economy, even had he actually done so, is no evidence that the discovery was due to that method or belongs to that school. It must first be proved by the claimants—the deductive school—that it is a legitimate deduction from some higher law. Now it certainly was not arrived at by deduction from the principle of differentiation regarded as one of the universal concomitants, or rather manifestations, of evolution, inasmuch as no such principle had at that time been formulated. Rather is it the case that physiology first, and, later on, philosophy itself, are indebted for this generalisation to the *Wealth of Nations.* To contend that such a principle could have been deduced from purely psychological data is as vague as it is ridiculous. Undoubtedly, when once arrived at by induction from observed facts, nothing is easier than to verify the conclusion by an appeal to psychological considerations, as was actually done by Adam Smith; just in the same way as geologists, when once they have ascertained certain truths concerning the nature and conformation of particular strata, show that such was all along a necessary result of the meteorological laws at work. What would be thought of any one who should contend that the law of natural selection is a deduction from psychological laws simply because the desire of animals to feed and to reproduce their kind is brought into the calculation? The doctrine of free trade is of course the result of the application of this principle of the division of labour to international exchanges; and since the authors of the *Logic of Political Economy* and of the *Plutology* agree in attributing to this doctrine the success of their science, the claims of the latter to our respect are already considerably diminished. Indeed, nothing is left which can bear comparison with that to which its title is denied.

Next in order of time and of merit comes the law of population as enunciated by Malthus.

As Adam Smith was the forerunner of Mr. Herbert Spencer, so Malthus is the precursor of Mr. Darwin. For without the demonstrated disparity between the geometrical increase of population and the harmonical increase of food, and the consequent struggle for existence, we could have had no theory of the origin of species by the survival of the fittest, unless, indeed, the eminent naturalist had been his own Malthus, which is far from improbable; for of all self-evident truths none seems now-a-days so obvious as this so-called Malthusian doctrine. It has been well said that every new truth, on its way to acceptation, passes through three stages: the first in which it is ridiculed as the craze of a madman, the second in which it is detested as the crotchet of a minority, and the third in which it is matter of wonder how it could ever have been disputed. Surely Malthus's heresy must have reached the third phase, for how it can ever have been doubted or carped at by sane men passes all understanding. However, the question for us to decide at present is how it was originally arrived at. If by deduction, from what higher law? Compare the following :—Achilles and a tortoise run a race; Malthus observes that Achilles runs considerably faster than the tortoise, and he concludes—mark! he concludes—that the tortoise will be left behind. In other words, population will outstrip means of subsistence; whereupon Malthus further concludes that since there is not enough for all, some must go without. Is this by deduction or otherwise? Again—this time, assuredly, by means of a rigid induction from experience—he concludes that those who go without food will starve. Now we are in possession of the three steps in his reasoning—first, an observed fact; second, a conclusion which is hard to put in the form of a syllogism; and third, an induction. There is something truly comical in the double claim of political economy to be a deductive science and at the same time prolific of successful results.

We have heard a great deal about these fundamental psychological laws from which all economical laws are said to be deduced. Where are they? What are they? We ought to have them enunciated at the head of every treatise so as to admit of reference. A careful search for them shall be presently instituted; but we must previously accomplish what we have taken in hand, and inquire into the method by which the third great triumph of political economy was reached—Ricardo's celebrated theory of rent. Now, as it happens, it was just because land obstinately refused to conform to his theories of capital and wages (standing forth as it did a grand contradiction of his conclusions) that he was driven to what his genius abhorred—observation. Nor is this said in disparagement of Ricardo's abilities or his work. Both are justly held in universal respect. The plain truth remains that, brought up in the Scotch school of thought, he was naturally prone to work out his theories *à priori*, and to pay insufficient attention to the facts on which they professed to be based. Still he was no blind metaphysician, shrieking " *Tant pis pour les faits*," and when his attention was drawn to the fact that the phenomena of rent did not conform to his theories, but, on the other hand, had all along been held up in triumph by the enemy, he determined to take the bull by the horns without further delay.

First he observes that farmers prefer cultivating inferior soils to investing beyond a certain amount in superior; and the reason of this he discovers to be that additional doses of capital applied to the same portion of land bring in proportionally smaller and smaller returns. This truth has been dignified with the title of "the law of diminishing returns," but when once shown to hold good, as Professor Hearn has shown, not only in the case of land, but of everything else, it better deserves the title of a "truism." Every additional pound weight placed on the top of half a lemon will express an additional quantity of juice; but after some thirty pounds have done their work it is but a sorry drop that your thirty-first will give you.

Ricardo next observes that while farmers' profits are tolerably proportional to the capital invested, rents, on the other hand, vary enormously, and, indeed, approximately, *cæteris paribus*, as the fertility of the soil. From these data it is easy to perceive how Ricardo evolved his theory of rent; and those who could regard it as a deduction must have an extraordinary conception of a syllogism.

I have now disposed of the claims of the deductive school of political economy to Adam Smith's principle of the division of labour, and its application to free trade, to Malthus's law of population, and to Ricardo's theory of rent. If there is any other discovery, real or supposed, to the credit of which they consider themselves entitled, such as the wage-fund, or the inverse ratio of wages and profits, or certain theories of value, or what not, to these and all such, so far as I am concerned, they are welcome. I know of no other school that even puts forward claims to any results whatever.

It still remains possible that, although nothing has

yet accrued to us as the result of the deductive method applied to the psychological treasures of which we are in present possession, a golden harvest is yet in store for us.

Although the glorious machinery kept in motion and superintended by a great school of economists, with Professor Fawcett at their head, and well stocked with the very best quality of psychological raw material, has up to the present produced nothing; although, in order to obtain the only three or four pieces of finished goods in the warehouse, Messrs. Smith, Malthus, and Ricardo were driven to stop the works, to bring in material from out-of-doors, and to work it up by hand —in spite of all this, we are bidden to sing "There's a good time coming." It may be so; wherefore let us, with all due diligence, examine our raw material —our "fundamental psychological data." I regret that I have not been able to find these laws stated by more than three writers; and these three, unfortunately, do not express them in precisely the same words, as is customary with the laws of motion and other important physical laws.

1st. "That every person will choose the greater apparent good."

2nd. "That human wants are more or less quickly satiated."

3rd. "That prolonged labour becomes more and more painful.

Here, then, are three of them as stated by Professor Jevons. "And thence," says he, "we deduce the laws of supply and demand, the nature and laws of that ambiguous conception, value, especially the laws governing its relation to labour or cost of production." (p. 24.) Professor Cairnes, who, after Senior and Mill, admits also physical data, gives us the following :—

"1st. The desire for well-being implanted in man, and for wealth as the means of obtaining it, and, as a consequence of this, in conjunction with other mental attributes, the desire to obtain wealth at the least possible sacrifice.

"2nd. The principles of population as derived from the physiological character of man and his mental propensities. And

"3rd. The physical qualities of the natural agents, more especially land, on which human industry is exercised."

Mill also informs us that political economy is based upon certain laws of matter and certain laws of mind. "The law of mind is, that man desires to possess subsistence, and consequently wills the necessary means of procuring it." "The laws of matter are those properties of the soil and of vegetable life which cause the seed to germinate in the ground, and those properties of the human body which render food necessary to its support." How laws can be properties, or what on earth could be deduced from such laws if they were laws, he does not explain. But in another work (*Logic*, vol. ii., p. 488) he says—" The psychological law mainly concerned is the familiar one that a greater gain is preferred to a smaller." "By reasoning from that one law of human nature

. . . . a science may be constructed which has received the name of political economy."

When the fundamental laws and psychological and other data are thus drawn out before us, shall we not, if we refrain from laughter, express our astonishment that men can be found capable of professing to build up a science on such a foundation—upon laws that are not laws, and upon commonplaces the very clothing of which in words renders them ludicrous?

One more small body of observations and discoveries remains to be accounted for and put in its proper place. Such are M. Chevalier's valuable conclusions concerning the fall in the value of the precious metals during recent times over and above the decline due to increased supply. This he very justly attributes, after ascertaining the fact from statistics, to the progress of civilisation and increasing credit. Gold is less prized as an ornament than it was among barbarous or semi-barbarous peoples; and money is no longer in Western Europe stored away in holes and corners by a suspicious and insecure people as is the case (though less and less as time flies) in India. Such, again, are some of Mill's inductions from an extensive survey of facts as to the comparative productiveness of different kinds of farming. He may have overlooked certain factors of the case, but, for all that, subject to correction, they are useful, standing, as they avowedly do, on the *terra firma* of observed facts. Such, again, are some of Professor Cairnes's notes on the effect of the gold discoveries, and of many suggestive observations of Professor Hearn.

But what is much to my present purpose is the fact that observations of this character were made, and even accounted for, before political economy was born. Witness the well-known tables of Gregory King, drawn up two centuries ago, in which he attempts, and with partial success, to find, by means of statistics, the proportion which holds between certain stated deficits in the supply of corn in England and the prices consequent thereupon:—

A deficit of 1-tenth raises the price 3-tenths.
,,   2   ,,   ,,   ,,   8   ,,
,,   3   ,,   ,,   ,,   16  ,,
,,   4   ,,   ,,   ,,   28  ,,
,,   5   ,,   ,,   ,,   45  ,,

Now all this and similar valuable information, whether obtained before or since the establishment of a so-called science of political economy, is merely evidence of the operation of a well-known principle in the history of sciences.

Not only did psychological truths spring up under the very noses of the metaphysical philosophers, but they themselves contributed to the accumulation, unwittingly, of positive facts which finally overwhelmed them and all their airy castles. Again, read the *Testimony of the Rocks*, and bethink you with what object it was written, and how marvellously it contributed to the destruction of that which it was intended to support; and, further, how terribly, like the monster in *Frankenstein*, it avenged its own creation.

Again, regard the worthy Dr. Paley collecting facts for his *Natural Theology*, and consider how admirably those very observations have been elaborated into the most crushing argument against the teleogical hypothesis. Have not our Hegels and those who aspire to re-think the great thought of creation been likewise driven to extract truths by observation from the annals of chroniclers which have eventually helped to establish positive history on a firm footing—just as though they could not have evolved all necessary truths out of the inexhaustible well of their own inner consciousness?

So is it with Plutology. Slowly and silently she has been growing up in our midst, uncared-for, unrecognised, but none the less waxing stronger and stouter, till now the time has come to put forth her claims to undisputed dominion over the phenomena of wealth, and, if need be, to challenge Political Economy to mortal combat.

A full description of this new aspirant to scientific honours will be given in the next chapter. The object of the present one has been, not, indeed, to bring to light the power of Plutology, but to expose the weakness and littleness of her reigning adversary. If in this attempt I have been successful, the reader will admit the needfulness of some such work as the succeeding portions of this book, and will at the same time remember that it is offered to the public by no means as a complete treatise on plutology, but merely as a preliminary step towards the establishment of that new science on a firm footing. And he will further remember that the difficulties and dangers which beset the innovation are very different from those which hampered the introduction of Philology and other recently-developed sciences, inasmuch as the latter had no "vested interests" to meet on the threshold—no well-established rival to dethrone.

The indictment consists of the following charges against political economy, being a summary of the above conclusions:—

Its advocates cannot agree as to whether it is a science at all, or whether it is not rather an art, like engineering. Neither are they at one as to its method, some contending that it is a deductive science, others that it is not. Some, again, say that it is an exact science; others that it is exact in theory, but being hypothetical, not exact in fact; and others, again, that it is not a mathematical or quantitative science at all, and therefore, *à fortiori*, not exact. From its nature to its method, from its method to its definitions, from its definitions to its very conclusions, these fundamental differences proceed, till there is not one single proposition or theory upon which one can stand and say, "This is *terra firma*."

Nor has it been admitted into the enchanted circle, the circle of the inductive sciences, that, ever growing hand in hand, mutually give and take assistance, bound together in one happy brotherhood. Political economy, I say, has no place in this circle. How should it? It has no settled rank. Is it concrete or abstract-concrete? Nobody knows.

Lastly, unlike any other science, it has incurred the hatred of certain classes of the community, especially of the working-man; and the contempt of practical statesmen and men of commerce. No invalid curses botany when his drugs do him no good; no shipwrecked mariner curses astronomy; no ruined stockbroker curses arithmetic; no victim of a railway collision curses mechanics; what, then, is this anomaly? Why is political economy, alone of all the sciences, assailed and set upon at all points? Why? Because it is not a science, and men of common sense see that it is not. It is a body of doctrines more or less arbitrary, like the dogmas of a creed, and as little entitled to respect as the feeblest of them. There is my answer; and if plutology, when once established, is similarly assailed, it will be time to admit that I am wrong.

## CHAPTER II.

### POSITION OF PLUTOLOGY.

No science can claim to be fairly launched until its relation with respect to the other sciences has been determined; its province clearly marked out; its functions allotted to it, and the limits of its jurisdiction carefully defined. The anomalous position of political economy, even when assumed to be a speculative science, has been already shown. In the present chapter I propose to determine the province of plutology, and to make room for it in a complete classification of the sciences—in other words, to define it.

It is not necessary to go back so far as to the nebulous period of the earth's history in order to reach a time at which, with perfect assurance, we may say that the existence of organic matter on its surface was an impossibility. Nor is it necessary for my purpose to enter into the needlessly-vexed question of spontaneous generation. It suffices to remember that the lichens, howsoever originated, which first mantled the exposed rocks, were necessary precursors of a higher vegetation. True as it is that plants are impossible without soil, it is equally true that soil is impossible without plants; and hence it is that it is often needful to sow furze and other weeds before the nobler and more useful orders of the vegetable kingdom can obtain foothold.

Little by little in the world's history, as the mould thickened and improved, first one and then another step was reached. After the lichens had paved the way the mosses were rendered posssible; after the mosses the ferns; and after the ferns the pines and other highly-organised orders.

As in similar cases, this mutual interdependence of existing things, each being the cause and effect of the other, appears to some a paradox. Professor Max Müller has maintained that language is the cause of thought, in opposition to others who have contended that thought is the cause of language: the truth being that, as in the case of soil and vegetation, each has grown *pari passu* with the other from the beginning by infinitesimal increments due to the action and reaction of each upon each.

Now there is a science much indebted to the late Professor Liebig which treats of soils, manures, permanent manures, irrigation and aëration of soils, the rotation of crops, and the like matters, and though usually studied only in connection with the art of agriculture, there seems no logical reason against its being raised to the rank of a speculative science, and considered apart from practical ends. Were this done, the science (let us call it Aialogy) would bear the same relation to botany that plutology bears to sociology.

Now soil might well be termed "transformed environment," for although necessary to the very existence of vegetation, it is altogether formed by it out of surrounding inorganic matter. Man also has his transformed environment, which it is now time to examine.

Suppose the whole human race annihilated, and a learned *savant* sent down from Saturn to examine and classify the productions of this earth and to carry back to his native planet a correct account thereof. Amongst the crystals in the caverns, the wild beasts and insects in the desert, the trees and shrubs in the Brazilian forest, the fishes in the sea, and the cuttings of extinct glaciers, he would feel quite at home. All would be natural and as would have been anticipated from known causes. But what are these? Symmetrical objects of stone and iron, but possessing no crystalline force competent to account for the complexity of the result. Would he not be perplexed with the houses, the barometers, the steam-engines, the ticking clocks, the strange collection of laminated structures which we call libraries? What gigantic spider can have woven these metal webs over the face of the earth, and even at the bottom of the ocean? These tunnellings, again, through the hills, and then these tall embankments across the valleys—these are not the result of glacial action. And yet further: quitting these anomalous specimens of inorganic matter, the mysterious agency penetrates into the vegetable and animal world. Here are plants bearing flowers with abnormally large petals, capriciously marked, and others bearing fruits with uselessly-enlarged parenchyma; and others, again, growing where they have not a chance of surviving. Here are animals in countless flocks and herds just beginning to be exterminated by other species from sheer inability to protect themselves against attack; while others are dying for the simple reason that they do not know how to take care of themselves, or to find the good things around them; here, in fine, are animals of many sorts utterly unfitted for the great struggle for existence. But, after all, it would be the inorganic varieties of this anomalous class which would present the most interesting and inexplicable spectacle to our supposed *savant*—the watches, the books, the locomotives, the paintings, the bridges, and the textile fabrics.

It is clear, without further enumeration, and dismissing our learned friend, that there does exist an enormous accumulation of what cannot be better described than as transformed environment—that is to say, of surrounding natural objects transmuted by man for his own benefit into something different from what they were before, and without which he could no more exist in his present numbers and civilisation than the vegetable kingdom could exist without soil. The analogy (nay, it is more than an analogy) between the vegetable and human environments may be conducted one step further.

We all know that vegetation has not only modified surrounding nature to a great extent, but has to an equal extent been modified by surrounding nature. By adapting themselves to the conditions in which they have found themselves, some plants have flourished and obtained nutriment from substances which others have been unable to assimilate, and have thereby survived to the exclusion of their rivals. To the power of absorbing and assimilating the carbonic dioxide of the air we owe the existence of the terrestrial flora; and, without further illustration, it is evident that another class of commodities exists useful to plants besides those which they have expressly created for themselves. Not only those substances (aluminum, calcium, silicon, &c.) which, by combining with other ingredients, plants have adapted for their own use but also those substances to which they have adapted themselves, fall into the category of utilities from a vegetable point of view.

So with man. By gradually fitting himself out when (say) in the ascidian stage with suitable air-chambers or lungs, he adapted himself to the conditions required of terrestrial animals, and thereby brought oxygen under the category of utilities. To water he had previously adapted himself; and, subsequently, one by one vegetable and animal substances were turned to account as nutriment, not by cooking or otherwise adapting *them*, but by changes effected in his own digestive apparatus.

Now clearly it matters not on which side the requisite adaptation took place; the end attained is the same—equilibrium. And the commodities thus rendered useful to man may be lumped together as utilities, or by whatever name it may be convenient to designate them. The term "wealth" is perhaps as suitable as any. At all events, the term "transformed environment" must be discarded, inasmuch as, although it well expresses the materials adapted to human nature, it excludes the materials to which human nature has adapted itself.

Adopting the term "wealth," then, the following is the definition of it:—Wealth is the general name for all those commodities which are useful to man. And it further appears that the origin of wealth is coeval with that of mankind, and has advanced together with it from generation to generation, each advance in the one rendering an advance in the other possible. Wealth is the makeweight without which man would not be in equilibrium with his surroundings.

Two observations, and two only, are requisite in connection with the above definition. The first is, whereas most writers prefer to say "useful or desirable," I, on the other hand, am content with the word "useful" alone; in the first place, because, in the absence of any general acceptation to the contrary, that which is desired by an individual is to the extent of pleasing him so far useful to him. Plutology cannot impose a moral connotation on the term. And in the second place, that which is desired by the individual, even though injurious to himself when obtained, may be presumed to be useful and beneficial to the race. Without straying too far into biological speculations, this point may receive a little attention. The fact that a desire exists is *primâ facie* evidence that its satisfaction is good for the race, else whence and how sprang the desire? Desires which tend to destruction or inferiority must perish with the desirers. Nor must we rashly infer that desired objects which have no apparent utility in them are therefore useless. "Upon the subject of human wants," says Bastiat, the most philosophical of economists, "I have to make an important observation, one which in political economy may even be regarded as fundamental; it is that wants are not a fixed, immutable quantity; they are not in their nature stationary, but progressive. Scarcely has a man found shelter than he desires to be lodged; scarcely is he clothed than he wishes to be decorated; scarcely has he satisfied his bodily cravings than study, science, art, open to his desires an unlimited field." And these remarks, be it noted, apply no less to the race than to the individual. Hence it is that we are justified in declining to point out the advantage to accrue to the race from the gratification of particular desires, on the ground that the stable equilibrium of future generations may, for aught we know, depend on the satisfaction of desires that we have never experienced or dreamt of, and of which the apparently meaningless whims and fancies of the wealthy classes may possibly constitute the incipient stage. At one end of that silken ribbon behold a small white hand glittering with diamonds; at the other a well-washed, plump Maltese terrier. In what sense, it is asked, can these things be said to satisfy the stable equilibrium of the owner or the race? We cannot tell. Again, it has been contended that man would be better off without than with a taste for spirituous liquors. Yet who shall say to what extent anæsthetics of one kind or another may not become absolutely requisite to future generations, when even now it is clear that human development is proceeding chiefly in the direction of nervous change?

Unaccountable cravings may, then, be an index to future satisfactions of the highest order.

The second observation on the above definition of wealth relates to a dispute which has been referred to in the preceding chapter. Without anticipating the consideration of the term "value," I will here re-state and consider the objections of those who quarrel with my definition on the ground that it is too wide. "It includes," say they, "both air and water. The utilities embraced in it should be only those which possess exchangeable value."

It does include air and water, and so it should. Perhaps the best argument wherewith to meet these disputants is the *reductio ad absurdum.*

Here are two tribes in an island in which nuts, berries, and edible roots are scarce and animals scarcer. But there flourishes in great abundance a succulent plant which when raw is indigestible and unpalatable, but pleasant and nutritious when boiled. One tribe understands and employs the boiling process; the other, being unacquainted with and afraid of fire, does not.

While the latter toil hungry all day in search of nuts and berries the former have enough and to spare. They spend their energies in ministering to their higher wants; their numbers increase; they invent new processes; they gradually become civilised, and in time exterminate their poorer rivals. Pardon!— I used the word "poorer." No—the boiling tribe, say my opponents, is not wealthier than the other, because, by hypothesis, such is the abundance of the succulent plant that it has no value whatsoever. Now, had this plant been rarer, they continue, so as to have given rise to competition for it among the members of the tribe who knew how to cook it, it would then have possessed exchangeable value, and therefore would have constituted a portion of their wealth. Hence, if ever you meet with such a tribe, you have but to steal or destroy nine-tenths of its staple food to render it comparatively wealthy. Is further argument required?

The definition of wealth being now finally settled, so far as the purposes of this work are concerned, we may turn to the definition of plutology. This science deals with relations of some kind subsisting between the kinds of wealth. Now there are two attributes in respect of which these kinds may be compared—with respect to their absolute quantity, and with respect to their utility or power to afford gratification. Or, having found these ratios, we may, if we please, compound them and compare their compound ratios. The standard units employed might be, for the quantity, pound weights, and for the utility some unit of pleasures which may be left to Professor Jevons to determine. The equation will then stand: —Utility of first article divided by its quantity equals utility of second article divided by its quantity and multiplied by $x$. And $x$ will be the compound ratio required.

Well, all this is very dry and very chimerical. Firstly, the absolute quantity of any commodity procurable is difficult if not impossible to ascertain; and secondly, no two persons experience equal pleasure from the same article; and if they did I cannot concur with Professor Jevons in believing that it will ever be measurable.

However, the question need not be discussed. Fortunately for us all and for the science of plutology, we are spared not only the trouble of finding either of these ratios, but even that of compounding the two. It is already done for us—done with a precision which is surpassed in exactness and delicacy by the results of no other concrete science.

Value is this ratio; and it is the thermo-electric pile of the plutologist. The slightest breath of news, even from another hemisphere, causes it to oscillate perceptibly; and, indeed, it is seldom, if ever, completely at rest.

Plutology, then, resolves itself into an inquiry into the uniformity of the relations of value subsisting between the forms of wealth.

Although no one who troubles to think can doubt whether certain things are or are not wealth according to the definition already given of it, yet such is the evil effect of loose thought and of habit, and such is the density of the clouds in which the conception has been enveloped, especially of late, that one warning word will not be out of place. It is this, that in all cases wealth denotes only concrete, tangible things —*bonâ fide* substances no more incorporeal than the stones on the road or the air we breathe.

Mr. McLeod—the theoretical part of whose work

is certainly less instructive, if more amusing, than the historical—divides wealth into three classes:—

"1st. Material products such as corn, manufactures, houses, &c., &c., which every one admits to be wealth. . . . .

"2nd. The economic quantities which may be summed up under the title of labour. . . . .

"3rd. The third species of economic quantities are, however, of a different nature. Intangible and invisible like the second species, they are yet transferable like the first; and when we exchange or sell them we divest ourselves absolutely of the property in them, as we do of the first species."

Under the last head he includes shares in public companies, copyright, instruments of credit, the public funds, &c., under the name of *incorporeal*. Beware of confounding thus rights and wealth. A promissory note is merely a promise to pay, and the paper on which such promise is recorded is no more entitled to be called wealth than the sound of an honest man's voice making the same promise. A patent, again, which is the exclusive right to make, use, exercise, or vend an invention, is not wealth. If it be, what becomes of it at the end of the fourteen years for which it is granted? A certain patented invention contributes to the production of an article of value. Part of the price received for it goes to the patentee and part to the manufacturer (supposing them to be two persons). Suddenly the patent is extinguished in a court of equity as an infringement. The value of the product is in no wise affected thereby, only the manufacturer retains the whole instead of a part of it. In fine, patent right, as the term implies, is merely a right to certain wealth which may be created; and unless we are prepared to regard all rights as wealth, we cannot consistently confer that title on patents or on any other form of what has received the name of incorporeal property—a name, by the way, which we owe to the unphilosophic nomenclature and procedure of English law.

With regard to Mr. McLeod's second division, it will be fully established in a subsequent chapter of the present work that it is based upon misconceptions as gross as those giving rise to his third. To begin with, labour is not an entity at all. Like vital force, it is merely a metaphysical creation. We can no more consistently speak of human labour as wealth than we can of the power of an engine or of the heat of a furnace. Indeed, not even Mr. McLeod's party (if he has a party) have yet been heard to enter the power or toil of their horses or asses in an inventory of their stock. Then why the labour (whatever it may mean) of men? No: just as we bestow the appellation "wealth," not on the power, but on the engine; not on the heat, but on the furnace and fuel; not on the toil, but on the horses and donkeys; so we must bestow it, not on the labour, but on the men and women who can do the work.

So disappear from the scenes, it is hoped for ever, Mr. McLeod's second and third species of wealth, and the first remains alone in possession of the field. Those who consider this digression superfluous may be consoled by the reflection that it may have removed a stumbling-block from the pathway of weaker brethren. The definition, of course, sufficed without comment.

I shall conclude this chapter by finding the place of plutology in a complete classification of the sciences. Plutology discards the consideration of all practical questions and devotes herself entirely to the investigation of the laws regulating the relations of value subsisting between those concrete articles comprehended under the category of wealth. Thus, firstly, she is a purely speculative science—that is, a science in the true sense of the word—and secondly, she is a concrete science, like mineralogy and botany, and lays no claim to the attention of the self-styled students of the moral sciences. Of the method of plutology I shall speak in the next chapter. Meanwhile, accepting Mr. Herbert Spencer's as the best table of the classification of the sciences yet drawn up, and turning to Table III., which contains the concrete sciences, we search in vain for the name of political economy. And no wonder! But we do find biology branching off into the science of the laws of the organic phenomena of structure (morphology) on the one hand, and of function on the other. The latter divides itself into physiology and psychology, dealing respectively with the internal and external relations. Psychology, again, is general or special, and the special is separate or combined. It is this last which, under the name of sociology, deals with the laws of the functions of human beings in combination.

I confess I do not admire this part of the table so much as the rest. Structure, after having been quitted at the separation of morphology and physiology, must here be re-introduced; otherwise we have no science dealing with the structure of society. However, taking things as we find them, sociology must now be split up into two distinct branches. It has been pointed out that, in the progress of mankind, two factors, or sets of factors, require to be considered; and there can be no doubt as to the expediency of considering them separately. Mankind and a special class of non-human substances, both inorganic and organic, act and react one upon another, and result in mutual adaptation. Either without the other would be out of equilibrium with surrounding nature. Both are necessary and essential to the existence of society. The former, or non-human factor, constitutes the province of plutology; the latter might, in contradistinction therefrom, be entitled anthropology; but in all probability it will retain the name of sociology proper. Much that has hitherto been considered as forming part of the domain of political economy will henceforth fall under the jurisdiction, not of plutology, but of sociology, such, for instance, as Malthus's theory of population and Adam Smith's principle of the division of labour. The precise nature of the science of plutology will be further elucidated as its method is defined and its resources developed.

At the same time, in a chapter devoted to the nature and objects of a science, a short digression which takes the form of grains of comfort to the typical Englishman will not be out of place. The said typical Englishman is, rightly or wrongly, reported to be averse to the study of any science which does not give promise of sooner or later bringing grist to the mill. He is essentially practical. Mechanics he tolerates, for the sake of engineering; astronomy, for the sake of navigation; chemistry, for the sake of medicine, manufacturing processes, and agriculture; geology, for the sake of mining. Now if plutology has no concern with practical matters, why need he trouble himself about it? For this reason: that, just as engineering is not mechanics, but is based upon it, so there is an art which, though not plutology, is based on plutology and cannot well advance without it. That art is practical economy as manifested in manufacture and trade. Every art is limited and kept back, or expanded and urged forward, by its cognate science. And hence it is that the industrial classes will do well, and by no means waste time, in the careful study of plutology.

## CHAPTER III.

#### METHOD OF PLUTOLOGY.

IMPORTANT evidence of the unscientific nature of political economy, as has already been shown, is the unsettled state of opinion as to its method; and the fact that the majority of leading authorities concur in regarding what Mill calls the "inverse deductive method" as the one applicable to it rather confirms this judgment than otherwise. With the single exception of the science of waelth, all the concrete sciences have passed through the premature-deductive phase, and are now classed together as the inductive sciences. Reliable truths of a considerable degree of generality having been obtained by this rational method, valuable deductions may be, and of course have been, derived therefrom. It is not deduction that one deprecates. It is the attempt at deduction before any reliable general truths exist from which to deduce.

When general laws have not been discovered they have frequently been invented. Such was the law that "Nature abhors a vacuum." She would do anything to avoid a vacuum. Water would rise to an indefinite height in a tube, contrary to its natural predilections, to avert this detested consummation. Somebody tries to raise water accordingly to a greater height than thirty feet, and lo! the whole edifice collapses. Nature exults in a vacuum. Down goes the law, down go all the deductions from it, and everything is to begin over again.

Some people will no doubt object that valuable truths have been elicited by deduction from higher and more general truths, even before the inductive method had been applied to the facts. It may be so; it is so. We are continually, from our infancy, unconsciously generalising, and from these generalisations we may and do deduce minor truths of more or less value. But this does not affect the statement that before marked progress can be made induction must precede deduction in the investigation of concrete phenomena.

On this point Dr. Whewell writes, " During a great part of such stationary periods we shall find that the process we have spoken of as essential to the formation of real science, the conjunction of clear ideas with distinct facts, was interrupted, and in such cases men dealt with ideas alone. They employed themselves in reasoning from principles, and they arranged, and classified, and analysed their ideas so as to make their reasonings satisfy the requisitions of our rational faculties. This process of drawing conclusions from our principles by rigorous and unimpeachable trains of demonstration is termed *deduction*. In its due place it is a highly-important part of every science, but it has no value when the fundamental principles upon which the whole of the demonstration rests have not first been obtained by the induction of facts, so as to supply the materials of substantial truth. Without such materials a series of demonstrations resembles physical science only as a shadow resembles a real object. To give a real significance to our propositions, induction must provide what deduction cannot supply. From a pictured hook we can hang only a pictured chain." (*Hist. Inductive Sciences.*)

It seems to me that the Ricardian premisses bear to the whole superstructure of political economy pretty much the relation which this pictured hook bears to the pictured chain. His division of the agents of production into land, labour, and capital is as arbitrary as Aristotle's division of materials into fire, air, water, and earth. It is obtained in a similar fashion, and results in equal error and confusion.

Be this as it may, plutology will pass through the inductive stage before presuming to aspire to the rank of a complete science. Ere long, however, generalisations of a high order may be looked for, and then, and not till then, will deduction be in place. Here around us are thousands, nay, myriads of values, or rather of things having values, but shifting, and all so obviously bound together, so manifestly varying one with another, as to leave no doubt in any thinking mind that they rise and fall in obedience to general laws which it is the plutologist's function to discover. And at this point we see how striking is the resemblance between the chemical and the plutological method. Granite, water, green vitriol, iron rust, potatoes, air, and a thousand other substances of endless variety, might have been collected and compared to all eternity without any one suspecting that they had one element in common, and only one. Without analysis the elements must ever have remained unknown, and chemistry could have had no existence.

So with the materials of wealth. You may put together and compare diamonds, pigs, cloth, tea, oranges, and deal planks till crack of doom without finding out why their values are what they are, or how it is that some vary together while others remain unaffected. In order to accomplish this we must have recourse to the greatest instrument of discovery ever wielded by man—analysis. And it is in the application of this key, this chemical method, to the phenomena of wealth that the chief novelty of this work consists. There is this difference between chemical and plutological analysis, that whereas the former can be actually performed so that from a given compound we can obtain the several elements of which it is composed; the latter, on the other hand, can never be accomplished in fact, although it can be as accurately ascertained. In chemistry, again, the synthesis is frequently a difficult or impossible task, while in plutology it is a matter of everyday occurrence. It is difficult to pronounce upon the comparative advantages of these two processes. The decomposition of a compound into its elements, and the combination of simple substances into a compound one, afford equally reliable information as to the constitution of the compound—equally reliable but not equally full. In this respect, as will be shown hereafter, plutology has the advantage.

And it possesses another great advantage.

If the specific gravity of oxygen, or carbon, or sulphur varied from time to time, whether pure or in combination, we should at once have a clue to the constitution of numerous compounds, for out of a hundred substances, seventy-three, say, remain stationary, twenty-seven sink in weight, in different degrees. Weighing the elements, sulphur alone is found to have lost a considerable proportion of its specific gravity. We rightly infer that the twenty-seven substances may be compounds of sulphur, and that the seventy-three others certainly are not.

Plutologists possess this admirable test.

Substances rise and fall in value, and when elementary substances sink their compounds sink with them in proportion to the share of their own value which is due to the elementary substance entering into their composition.

With such a test can we not afford to be exact?

Shall plutology now be content to rank with mineralogy, and meteorology, and old political economy (regarded as a science), as a merely logical science—a science unfitted for mathematical precision? And if mathematical shall it be a mere science of more or less, like chemistry before the time of Lavoisier? Shall it not rather be an exact science?

"Space is measurable," writes Mr. Herbert Spencer, "hence geometry; force and space are measurable, hence statics; time, force, and space are measurable, hence dynamics. The invention of the barometer enabled men to extend the principles of mechanics to the atmosphere, and aërostatics existed. When the thermometer was devised there arose a science of heat which before was impossible. Such of the sensations as we have not yet found modes of measuring do not originate sciences. We have no science of smells, nor have we one of tastes. We have a science of the relations of sounds differing in pitch, because we have discovered a way to measure them, but we have no science of sounds in respect to their loudness or their *timbre*, because we have got no measures of loudness and *timbre*."

So a science (a quantitative science) of the relations of values is clearly a possibility, because we have a measure of values, perfect at any given time, and fairly trustworthy for purposes of comparison at different dates if used with care and reasonable correction.

Plutology, then, is a concrete science, an inductive science, an exact science; and to the requirements of such must its method correspond.

The plutologist's object is clear enough. His process should be no less so. His first step is one of common observation. He surveys the field of valuables, and notes down their respective values. But since this is certainly a herculean task he exercises his skill in selection, and chooses those substances which seem at first sight to possess the least in common. So far from gliding over extreme cases—cases which look like exceptions to any general laws—as the political economist does, these, on the contrary, he particularly seeks out and studies. Such are rough diamonds, town's water, land, coal under the surface, slaves, &c., and they have long been the acknowledged extreme cases, exceptions, and, in fine, bugbears of the economist.

His next endeavour is to classify his specimens on some uniform system after the example of the older sciences. Naturalists no longer class together pigs and sheep as domestic, or elephants and bears as big, or whales and salmon as marine. The pig and the elephant go together now-a-days, because they are more nearly related by blood than the pig and the sheep; and the whale is taken out of the water to be classed with his relatives the terrestrial mammals.

So the vegetable kingdom is not divided into tall trees and small plants, but the creeping strawberry falls with the tall apple-tree, and the bushy laurel under the head of Rosaceæ, simply because they are reasonably supposed to have all descended from a common ancestor, possibly enough unlike any of them. The genealogical relation is found to be the appropriate basis of classification.

Nor does the plutologist content himself with an inferior classification. In order, then, to discover the appropriate characteristics of his various specimens of wealth he must next proceed to their careful analysis, very justly surmising that the classes arranged on the best plan are more likely to be found respectively obedient to general laws, and to possess properties common to themselves and peculiar, than classes formed on any other system of classification. In this surmise he is justified by the example of the other sciences.

Lastly, he proceeds to discover certain laws of value, and then ascending and descending he ascertains those which cover more and less ground, till he arrives at some valuables which appear to obey in their variations, in addition to the more general laws, certain important laws to which few, if any, other species seem to be subject. There is no reason why he should stay this process until he has educed the individual peculiarities of every valuable under the sun; but though this will doubtless be accomplished, it is the business of the special trades thus to fill in the detail of the outlines which it is the plutologist's province to sketch. Of course the analysis will have to be verified by comparison with the actual synthesis, the cause of the several steps of which will require explanation before our task is complete.

Not till all this is accomplished shall we find ourselves in a position to predict from given data the future rise or fall in the price of any commodity to a nicety; and even then, as in astronomical calculations, the accuracy of our results will depend entirely on the caution with which we take into account known disturbing causes. From false data we cannot expect true conclusions, and if by accident or neglect we fail to observe certain tendencies in the prices of commodities involved in the calculation we have in hand, we shall of course to that extent fall short of or fly beyond the mark.

This is no sufficient reason for stigmatising plutology as a merely hypothetical science, as some would appear to think. Nothing can be more precise than the accuracy with which a chemist can predict the weight of the precipitate resulting from the mixture of given weights of certain solutions. Theoretically he can tell to the millionth part of a grain, but in practice he may find that owing to the impurity of an acid, or the imperfect solution of a salt, his calculations are some grains wrong. Would any one therefore describe chemistry as a hypothetical science? Furthermore, if a similar discrepancy between the actual and the predicted value occur over and over again, it may end by bringing to light a new law or a hidden fact; as the error in the calculated velocity of sound suggested to Laplace the generation of heat in its transmission. Let us not despair, then, if our predictions are not at first quite so satisfactory as we could have hoped.

## CHAPTER IV.

### THE DATA OF PLUTOLOGY.

BEFORE proceeding to consider the plutological analysis referred to in the last chapter there are certain data which require our previous attention. I describe these facts as data, not because they are actually axiomatic or inexplicable, but simply because the plutologist must accept them as facts without inquiring into their cause. Their explanation belongs to those sciences which I have ventured to class together as the anthropological sciences proper.

First of all it is to be observed that everything of value owes its value entirely to the desire of man. Without such desire or want nothing could have value, no matter what the cost of its production. Hence it is that certain facts concerning the wants of man require noting down—noting down, but that is all. No evil should be more carefully guarded against by writers on scientific subjects than that of trespassing beyond the boundaries of their own lawful domain. Such a practice, frequent as it is, leads to waste of energy on the one hand and to immature opinions on difficult and important questions on the other. In this chapter I shall endeavour to avoid following the example of the economists in the discussion of questions which rightly appertain to jurisprudence and psychology.

As matter of fact it is to be observed that the wants of man are manifold and of various intensities. The satisfaction of them is, we are told by biologists, the satisfaction of the conditions of our equilibrium.

Certain of these conditions are so imperative that their non-satisfaction results in unstable equilibrium even to the extent of complete dissolution. The articles which satisfy these paramount wants are called the necessaries of life—such as food and clothing.

From these upwards we find wants of every degree of urgency. Necessaries of life obtained, bare comforts are demanded. Then there arises a desire for luxuries, and then for dainties, and lastly for the refinements and fancies of high life.

"Man wants but little here below," writes the poet, but few who will make a careful inventory of the objects required to render happy the several grades of society, from the beggar cringing for a morsel of dry crust to the china-fancier bartering his thousands for a bit of pot, will sum up his conclusions in the same words.

The things or commodities which satisfy these multifarious wants are called utilities, a term which, for want of a better, I shall adopt. Thus the air we breathe, the water we drink, the bread we eat, the clothes we wear, the house we dwell in, the books we read, the fiddle we scrape, the pictures we hang on our walls, &c., &c., are all utilities.

We have seen that these utilities are of all degrees with respect to their utility or desirability, from those which quench the fire of thirst to those which satisfy a want which is hardly felt; they also are of all degrees in respect of another attribute, likewise of great importance. They are all limited in quantity, but in different degrees. Even the air we breathe is limited. So are diamonds the size of the Koh-i-noor. But what a contrast in the degree of their limitation! The former is so abundant as to be procurable at all times, in all places, and to any required amount, gratis and without effort; the latter can be counted on the fingers of one hand, and are not to be had for the asking. Between these two are utilities of every degree of limitation. Water costs nothing in the country, a little in most towns, and a great deal too much for the ratepayer's patience in London. Sometimes, as travellers tell us, it will fetch more than a guinea a pint in the Sahara. Bread is obtained in great quantities in most parts of the world. Meat is much rarer in this country. Oranges are so abundant as to be had for nothing in Brazil, and apples in Devonshire. Deal is more abundant than oak, iron than gold, Italian than Greek marbles, Scotch terriers than British mastiffs. The very surface of the land we live in is limited to so many thousand square miles. In fine, without further illustration, what is to be noted is that all things (whether utilities or not) are limited to a greater or less extent from the *practically-unlimited* to the *extremely-rare*.

Nor is there any connection whatever between their degree of utility and their degree of limitedness (if I may use such a hideous expression). We have, on the contrary, commodities rare and useful, rare and useless, abundant and useful, and abundant and useless.

The next fact which requires observation is the institution of property. The greater part, if not the whole, of the world's utilities we find in the possession of individuals, and the rest of mankind is excluded from participation in the enjoyment of them. Why this appropriation is tolerated and even supported by mankind is not for us to discuss. Such is the fact. Plutology accepts it as a datum.

Without property or ownership, in their widest signification, there could clearly be no exchange. Ownership established somehow—by law or by individual might—is pre-requisite to exchange. Man alone exchanges—that is, he gives up that which is his for that which is another's.

Most voluntary exchanges are mutually advantageous—each prefers that which belongs to his neighbour to that which he himself possesses. A has two coats and no cow, B two cows and no coat. B cannot drink more than the milk from one cow, and, moreover, he is very cold. A finds himself too hot in two coats, and thirsty withal. What more natural than to exchange one cow for one coat? Each now possesses one cow and one coat. It is possible that a third party, C, may come to B and say, "Do not give A your cow for a coat; see: I will give you a coat and also a hat for your cow." And so, without further exemplification, a system of recognised exchanges is established by competition, which regulates the amount of any commodity for which any other commodity may be obtained in exchange. This ratio is known as the value of the one commodity in terms of the other; and when all values are reduced to a uniform scale the value of any article expressed in terms of the recognised standard is termed its price.

It is needless to observe that gold is the standard in this and most other European countries; silver and gold in France and some others; and silver in some of the countries of the East. The price of an article is, in plain English, its value expressed in money.

A good deal of nonsense has been written apparently with a view to obscure the simplicity of the notion value. Economists seem to find every now and then so much of ease and commonplace about their science, that, like theologians, they are driven for the maintenance of their dignity to kick up a dust and proclaim a mystery within the cloud. Surely with some such object Professor Jevons has warned his readers against that dangerous term "value." "Value," it is said, "is a ratio and not an entity; it is the ratio of the amount of one thing to the amount of all other things for which it can be exchanged; not of *any* but of *all* other things. You must not say that the value of a sack of coals is three hundredweight of pig-iron, for so to speak is to make a piece of iron, which is an entity, the value of a sack of coals, which is, or should be, a ratio." I mention all this sophistry merely to warn the reader against it. Value is clearly a relative term, and you cannot express the value of a thing except in terms of some other thing. The value of a sack of coals *is* three hundred weight of pig-iron, and its price is twelve shillings and sixpence. In terms of butter its value is ten pounds of butter. In terms of hats its value is half a Lincoln and Bennett's silk hat, and so on. To speak of value as absolute instead of relative is absurd, and although we often speak of the value of a certain article as risen without reference to any specified commodity, we always in that case mean in relation to the majority of other commodities so far as our observations have extended. Most of the objections urged against the use of the term "value" apply with equal force to the term "weight." If value is a relation, so also is weight. Is there anything more anomalous in expressing the value of one thing in plain terms of another than there is in similarly expressing its weight? We do not hesitate to say that the weight of a pint of mercury is twelve pints of water. If we prefer to express it in pounds, ounces, and grains, we are merely falling back on the standard, as we do when we give the money value or price of an article.

So much for this verbal controversy. There is, however, a point of real importance in connection with price which requires a word. It is this: that whereas the relative weights of bodies never vary from century to century (though of their absolute weight we know nothing), in the case of values variations are of annual, daily, and hourly occurrence. Gold and silver form, of course, no exceptions to this rule. It is a difficult matter to ascertain what percentage of its value in relation to the majority of articles gold has lost during the last dozen years. The results of the calculations of several who have attempted to settle the point differ considerably. But there is no difficulty in showing that during that period silver has lost about 13½ per cent. of its value with respect to gold. If gold has lost 25 per cent., as some conjecture, in relation to most articles, then silver must have lost considerably more. This shows the folly of stating that bread, coals, meat, &c., have become dearer of late without first allowing for the fall in gold. If gold is cheaper everything else will be at a higher price. All this is very tedious because very stale, but in a work like the present it is frequently safer to re-state what is well known than to leave oneself open to misrepresentation.

A few further remarks open to like strictures may not, therefore, be deemed out of place.

First of all, it is not all utilities that have value.

Air is useful to the extent of being one of the prime necessaries of life; yet it has no value. No one will give anything for the air which anybody may appropriate, because he can obtain abundance elsewhere. Hence nobody cares to appropriate it, and it has no value. To possess value an article must be practically—that is, perceptibly—limited in amount.

Yet, again, not all things that are practically limited in amount have value. Mosquitoes are, or were, extremely rare in this country, yet so valueless are they that the proprietors of the Westminster Palace and Grosvenor Hotels will allow any one to take away all that they possess gratis; and it is probable, therefore, that their importation would not be attended with commercial success.

In order to possess value both these attributes must be combined. Every valuable commodity is a practically limited utility.

Surely after this it is almost superfluous to caution the reader against confounding value and utility. In vulgar parlance, it is true, an old man in a cottage is lauded for regarding his Bible as more valuable than all his furniture, whereas the former cost ninepence and the latter ten pounds. The bare caution is sufficient without expatiating on the distinction between value in use and value in exchange. These expressions have long ago slipped out of technical employment.

While on the subject of definitions, too, it may be noted that utility is not intended to convey any moral connotation. The toy for pleasure and the spade for work are equally useful in the plutologist's eyes, and but for circumstances to be explained in a future chapter, the term "gratificables" would be far superior for my purpose to "utilities." (See page 72.)

Another rather obvious proposition with regard to value is that there cannot be a general rise or fall in values. This needs no proof. One might as well set to work to prove that it is inconceivable that every man in the land should grow an inch taller than his neighbours.

Nor is the proposition which has been enunciated in a previous chapter more difficult to demonstrate— viz., that the sum of the values of the commodities in the world can be no measure of its wealth. For if we see that, other things equal, the value of an article connotes its scarcity as well as its utility, the absurdity of using a measure of scarcity as a measure of abundance is manifest.

It has been shown that the various kinds of utilities are capable of affording gratification of every degree; also that they exist in every degree of abundance. So, too, it has been pointed out that the requirements of every individual human being are of every degree of intensity and urgency. It remains only to add the familiar fact that property is distributed amongst mankind most unequally—in fact, in all degrees, from the slave who possesses absolutely nothing to the richest man with his million sterling a year.

Between the two extremes we find a graduated scale of wealth. It is not to be supposed that the gradations are regular and equal; that if there are a million persons with an income of £50 a year there are also a million with £100 a year, and so on till we come to the last of the twenty millions in this country at £1,000. On the contrary, the income-tax returns show a very different state of things.

Very interesting would be a diagram consisting of rectangular co-ordinates with mathematical curves showing the distribution of wealth in different countries. This could easily be obtained for all countries having an income-tax. The ordinate would represent the incomes in steps, say, from £20 per annum up to the highest income which is received by a considerable number of persons; and the abscissa would register the number of persons receiving the respective incomes.

Considerable light would be thrown by the superposition of these curves on the social construction of different countries. It would be extremely useful for purposes of trade, and still more so for fiscal purposes. Politicians might make capital out of it also, but that is of little importance.

I hope either to effect this object or to see it done by others before long. The way in which these curves would throw light on commercial operations will become evident when we have mastered the doctrine of value and supply.

To summarise the observations of this chapter, we have admitted certain data.

> First. The fact that human wants are of every degree of urgency, from hunger to a mere whim or fancy.
>
> Second. That commodities are of every degree of utility, from food to old broken china.
>
> Third. That all commodities are limited, but in different degrees, from the air we breathe to monster diamonds. And between these two latter attributes there exists no fixed relation.
>
> Fourth. The institution of property was admitted.
>
> Fifth. The fact that human beings exchange their properties frequently with mutual advantage.
>
> Sixth. It appears that competition results in fixed ratios of exchange which are called values.
>
> Seventh. That a uniform standard has been adopted,

and the value of any commodity expressed in terms of this standard is called its price.

The fluctuations in all values must be borne in mind, including that of gold, and a general rise of prices was shown to be not only possible but actual, while a general rise of values was shown to be absurd; as also the employment of value as a measure of the world's wealth.

Eighth and last. Wealth was admitted to be distributed in every degree of inequality amongst mankind; and a system of superimposed mathematical curves was suggested as a useful contribution to plutology.

## CHAPTER V:

#### COMBINATION.

It has been said that all utilities, and, *à fortiori*, everything of value, must possess the power of affording gratification—must satisfy some desire; and for this reason it was suggested that some term connoting this attribute would be better than the adopted term "utilities." A reason for rejecting the proposed change was promised in a future chapter. It is this:—Although all utilities are such in virtue of their power to afford gratification, yet the statement requires qualification to render it absolutely accurate.

Are there not many articles, it may be asked, which afford no pleasure whatever? A hammer for example. No one professes to derive pleasure from a hammer.

This brings us at once to the great division of utilities into directly-gratificable and indirectly-gratificable. The value of the hammer is due, not to its power of affording immediate pleasure, but to its power of assisting in, or causing the creation of, some other thing which can afford immediate pleasure. Or it may be that the hammer is used only for breaking a bar of iron or for fashioning a horseshoe, which in its turn again is not immediately pleasure-giving.

But the shod horse does at length afford direct gratification to the hunting man. Unless, sooner or later, pleasure is expected to be derived from a given article, mediately or immediately, that article can have no value. So that our original position is maintained, and pleasure, either proximate or ultimate, must be derivable from every commodity in order that it may possess value. In many cases, no doubt, there are almost endless degrees of remoteness from the final or pleasure-giving stage, as, for example, in the case of the hæmatite ore in the Lincolnshire fields, which is converted into pig-iron in the blast furnaces of the North. It is valuable as it lies in the fields, but after issuing from the furnace it is still more valuable to the maker of wrought iron or of steel; and after puddling, hammering, and other processes, it reaches the hands of the carriage-builder. Still, though considerably augmented in value, it is incapable of affording gratification; but after leaving his manufactory in the shape of a painted phaeton it gives direct satisfaction both to the comfort and the pride of the lady who drives it in the park.

Some commodities are capable either of affording direct gratification or of entering into the composition of other utilities; as, for example, coals. The same ton of coals may be burnt for the sake of giving warmth to the assembly in your drawing-room, or they may be used for fuel to boil the water that drives the engine, that turns the machinery, that spins the yarn, that forms the warp in the coat you wear.

In either case, when once used it is done with—

consumed. And so with the carriage, though not so quickly. At present what it behoves us to notice is that, sooner or later, everything is consumed that gives pleasure. Even the hammer is worn out in time, and a new hammer is worth more—other things the same—than an old one. During every process of manufacture everything which contributes to the creation of the new product is either entirely consumed, as the coals are in converting ore into iron, or merely deteriorated—that is, partly consumed, as a file is in sharpening chisels. No doubt a file may be used during several or many processes, but sooner or later it is worn out, and, as a file, valueless. Ultimate consumption is the fate of all indirectly-gratificable commodities, as of everything else, even the "eternal hills." They are, as it were, merged as to their value in the new product.

The difference between the durability of different indirectly-gratificable commodities is merely one of degree, a fact upon which Mill has laid great stress, even to the extent of classifying them according as they serve for one process or for more than one. The former he classes as "circulating capital," and the latter as "fixed capital." This somewhat unwarrantable distinction is difficult to follow. It is not very clear whether the candles lighting the mill serve for one process or two. All depends on the length of the candle and the length of the process. Soap, again, as employed by the laundress, suffices for several series of clothes; but when can the process be said to be over and a new process to begin? Some manures, too, are classed as fixed and others as circulating capital (and rightly so), but it would be hard to prove that the organic manures serve but one crop. Indeed, several crops in rotation get the benefit of one good application of organic manure. Again, on the other hand, take the cotton wick of an oil lamp used in illuminating a factory. When is the first process complete? Suppose we say when the factory closes. The wick may be consumed, but is it "circulating capital?" The emery paper used in polishing steel is completely consumed in a single process; but is it "circulating capital?" And so on.

And yet there is a difference—a fundamental difference, which is not one of degree, but absolute—between commodities according to the nature of their consumption. And this difference nearly corresponds with that upon which economists have based the distinction between fixed and circulating capital. I have taken files as an example of articles which may be used for more than one process before entire consumption. I have taken soap as another. But between these two there is a great gulf. The soap falls into one category with the coals used in a blast furnace, while the files fall into another with the furnace itself.

Let me endeavour to point out the fundamental distinction between these two classes. We are told (Mill's *Principles*, vol. i., p. 114), " Of the capital engaged in the production of any commodity there is a part which, after being once used, exists no longer as capital; is no longer capable of rendering service to production, or at least not the same service, nor to the same sort of production. . . . Capital which in this manner fulfils the whole of its office in the production in which it is engaged by a single use is called circulating capital. . . . Another large portion of capital, however, consists in instruments of production of a more or less permanent character, which produce their effect, not by being parted with, but by being kept, and the efficacy of which is not exhausted by a single use. . . . Capital which exists in any of these durable shapes, and the return to which is spread over a period of corresponding duration, is called fixed capital."

This division of capital into two classes, according as it serves for one process, or more than one, has led Mill and his followers into some very singular predicaments; but the fact is, that although in the majority of cases perhaps circulating capital is consumed in one process, while fixed capital (to employ this barbarous nomenclature) endures for several or many, such an observation is altogether immaterial for scientific purposes.

The true distinction lies much deeper, and is of great importance, as will hereafter appear. Circulating capital is properly defined as that which is essentially consumed, fixed capital as that which is accidentally consumed. Those things the eventual consumption of which (after no matter how many processes) is essential to the creation of the required product form one class. Those things the eventual consumption of which is not essential, but a mere accident of their nature, form another class. The iron ladle required for stirring the molten metal soon wears out, and must be renewed. If it wore out in a single use as the wick of a candle is destroyed, *pari passu*, with the tallow, it would be none the less accidentally consumed. Why? Because if it never wore out at all, even after a million processes, so far from being less useful in the production of refined silver, it would, on the contrary, rather render it more pure, and at the same time less costly.

So with the wick, I will not say in a candle, but in an oil lamp. It would be better if it never wore out at all; and so with a file, and so with a hammer and an engine. But not so with the oil. If that did not burn there would be no light; if coals were not consumed there would be no heat. Both oil and potash cease to exist as such when the soap is made. Their existence merges into that of the new product, and necessarily so. So, again, the woollen cloth is not manufactured without great cost in raw wool, and also in machinery; but whereas the consumption of the wool is clearly a *sine quâ non*, the wear and tear of the machines is a mere accident, and rather to be deplored than otherwise.

I think the distinction must be now pretty clear. To re-state: the number of processes for which any commodity will serve is merely a matter of degree, and consequently constitutes a distinction upon which no philosophical classification can be based such as can safely be founded upon the difference between essentially-consumed and accidentally-consumed commodities.

And now be it noted that this broad distinction

runs through the whole kingdom of valuables, not being confined to those articles which are known, or supposed to be known, as capital. Directly-gratificable commodities are likewise subdivided into two groups according as their eventual consumption is essential to their pleasure-giving, or merely accidental.

An apple to be enjoyed must be eaten, and is thus consumed. "A thing of beauty is a joy for ever" on the other hand, and the ravages which Time has made on the marble treasures of Hellas were not necessary to render the enjoyment of them possible. On the contrary, their power of affording satisfaction is thereby rather deteriorated than otherwise. All this is so obvious as hardly to require illustration when once pointed out.

To return to indirectly-gratificable commodities, a new case of identity presents itself. A very old and common distinction has always been perceived to exist between the essentially and the accidentally consumed elements of production—perceived, but dimly, and only when the contrast between the two is extreme, as between raw cotton and machinery. If you ask a working-man whether the town's water used in the boilers forms part of the tools or of the materials of the manufacture, he is put to his shifts to answer. And when you put similar questions in chemical works, dye works, &c., and on farms, the replies become more and more vague. Tools and materials are properly identical with essentially-consumed and accidentally-consumed indirectly-gratificable commodities. If the definitions are clearly borne in mind perhaps the vulgar terms are better than the more scientific, being less cumbrous; but the definitions *must* be remembered.

The horse which draws the plough, like the engine which performs the same process, would doubtless be all the more useful if he never wore out. Yet not only does he eventually wear out altogether, but at the end of even an hour or two becomes what is called fatigued, and unless he be repaired—that is, rested—is good for no more work, no matter how much food (fuel) you put into him. In this respect, then, he is unlike the engine, that the repairs necessary to keep him in order (for a large part of his food goes, not to the muscles only, but to keep him in general health) constitute a very large fraction in the expense of horse-work, though not so large a fraction as would justify political economists in disregarding all the other elements in the cost except that of repairs only. Nor, indeed, are they so blind as to do this, at least not in the case of horses; but in a parallel case, a case in which the absurdity is even greater, strange to say they do commit this extraordinary blunder, one and all.

Suppose you want a piece of land-ploughing by machinery. You hire a working engine. If the owner's charges are kept down by competition, or he is an honest man, you pay him a certain reasonable sum per day or hour for the use of the engine. Of the cost of the coal, oil, &c., employed, you need not trouble yourself. But if on inquiry you find that you have been charged more than the price of these articles you are not astonished. You very naturally admit that you must pay something towards the purchase-money of the engine, something towards its repairs, and something towards the rent of the shed in which it is kept dry, together with something towards minor incidental expenses.

Suppose you hire a horse by the hour instead. You expect to pay not only for his food consumed during the process, but also for the time during which he rests after the work, and a considerable amount towards repairs and risks, besides something towards the purchase-money, towards his stabling, attendance, &c., &c. There is nothing strange about all this. Even a political economist would pay up without a murmur.

But once bring man upon the scene in the capacity of worker or engine, and all other ordinary observations are lost sight of. Everything is turned topsy-turvy. There is a grand theory of wages and a wage-fund. Labour and capital and other glorious mysteries are flung about till bewilderment succeeds to common sense; ordinary mortals shake their heads and skulk away, leaving political economists in possession of the field to fight it out among themselves; and a pretty keen fight, it must be admitted, they make of it.

In considering the cost of horse-work we call to mind first the expenses incurred previous to his birth, which, as breeders know, are considerable; then his keep during the two or three years that "he was eating his head off" in the paddock; then when he enters upon his career of usefulness, besides his food, there is the rent of his stable, the time and trouble of grooming and attending to him, and, above all, the great risk of his falling lame or otherwise losing the whole or part of his value—a risk which is of course infinitely greater than in the case of an engine.

And what about the cost of man? Fifteen years at least, on an average, must elapse before a child can earn even its own living; and during all that period, besides the cost of food, fuel, clothing, and shelter, an immense outlay is required for an education of a more or less technical character, according to the business or profession for which he is intended.

"Man," says McCulloch, "is as much the product of previous outlays of wealth expended upon his subsistence, education, &c., as any instrument constructed by his agency. Every individual who has arrived at maturity, though he may not have been instructed in any particular art or profession, may yet with perfect propriety be viewed in relation to his natural powers as a machine which it has cost twenty years of assiduous attention and the expenditure of a considerable capital to construct. And if a further sum be spent in qualifying him for the exercise of a business or profession requiring unusual skill, his value will be proportionally increased; and he will be entitled to a greater reward for his exertions, as a machine becomes more valuable when it acquires new powers by the expenditure of additional capital or labour on its construction."

A man who should be able to work incessantly without fatigue, like an engine, would be a more valuable tool than a labourer of the ordinary type. In other words, the consumption of human beings, as elements in production, is not essential, but an accident of their nature.

Now a working engine and a working man each contains three important elements. First, there is the fuel which keeps the engine working, but not required for sustaining it when at rest. To this, *part* of the food of the working man corresponds. Then there are the commodities employed in repairing the engine, to which correspond the remaining part of the working man's food and other commodities necessary to *re-creation*. Finally, there is the original cost of the engine as it is, and of the man as he is. Both also require shelter, &c., which may be lumped with the repairs.

Is it not strange, then, with these very obvious analogies before them, that all economists have, as it were, entered into a conspiracy to disregard in their calculations by far the most important, if not the largest, item in the cost of labourers? Although both Adam Smith and McCulloch have noticed the importance of this outlay in the production of labourers, and the latter has gone so far in the passage just quoted as to compare them with machines—in spite of all this, in all calculations of the cost of production of articles created with the assistance of labourers, the labourers themselves are invariably left out of the reckoning, and the cost of the food, &c., required for their support alone considered. To me this is the most remarkable fact in the whole chapter of economical history. And yet it is a fact, and one which will receive a more prominent notice in the chapter on analysis. At present all we are concerned to note is that man is a tool entering as an element into the cost of production of other commodities just as an engine does.

Man, then, it appears, is regarded by the plutologist in two quite distinct aspects—firstly in his capacity of demander, and secondly in his capacity of labourer. In the former he is the cause of values; in the latter he is the part-cause of most valuables. This double rôle of man is of the utmost consequence, and, above all things, we must beware of confounding the two or of failing to keep them apart. Dreadful indeed have been the consequences of disregarding this fact, more especially because the two capacities very frequently inhere in the same individual, when it is more than ever of importance to avoid entangling their respective effects.

Or either of them may inhere separately. For instance, a slave having no property whatever, not even in his own body, cannot be a demander; but he is a labourer, and as such an element of the product he helps to create.

A gentleman, in the legal sense of one who lives on his means without working at anything, is a demander, but not a labourer; while a free working man, whether he be a tinker or a poet, combines the two, and thereby is a cause of values and a part-cause of valuables.

But in the exercise of these two functions the plutologist is bound to regard him as two distinct persons, in every respect as fully as though he actually were resolved into a slave on the one hand, and an idle gentleman on the other. This position must be firmly held before further progress is possible. The free labourer without other visible means of subsistence—that is, without other property—differs from a slave in this respect, that he is the proprietor of his own body—the proprietor of a slave who happens to be himself. This body, endowed as it is with the most extraordinary powers, is indeed a valuable possession; but of course of every degree of value in different individuals according to their abilities. In estimating a man's real wealth, then, we ought never to overlook (and practically we never do) that most important item, himself; and just as, out of several horses, this one, the winner of the Derby, is worth so many thousands of guineas, while that one dragging a four-wheeler will barely fetch a five-pound note in the open market; so, amongst men, of three, otherwise penniless, one is appointed to the governorship of Madras, with a salary of some thousands a year; a second obtains employment in a mechanic's shop at thirty shillings a week; while the third goes to the workhouse or dies of starvation. In practice I say this item is taken into consideration. When a father gives his daughter in marriage to a briefless barrister, dependent on an allowance from home, his justification is that "the fellow will get on; he has brains."

Without encroaching on the province of the sociologist I may here remark that experience has proved the economy of vesting the property of every man's person in himself; and, rightly or wrongly, the law of most civilised countries refuses to recognise the transfer of such property in the form of a sale out and out. Men do, however, let themselves out for hire at a fixed charge per hour, day, week, month, or year, and even for periods of seven years, just as they might let out their horses or engines. And just as a proprietor stipulates that his corn-crusher shall be used only for crushing corn, and not for crushing any other substances; so a free labourer, before agreeing to accept wages for his services, hedges himself round with certain conditions. The man who lets himself out by the month as butler only undertakes to perform certain services, to the exclusion of all others; and although within those limits he transfers his property in his own body to another for the time, it must not be supposed that this gives the transferee the right to do what he likes with him, or to exact more than certain specified services, any more than a similar bargain confers unlimited rights over a hired horse or corn-crusher.

One word, before returning from this digression, on the use of the terms *property* and *proprietor*. I willingly admit the charge of wresting these terms from their strict technical meaning. Jurists themselves employ them, however, with a wide and a narrow signification; in the former as synonymous with ownership (itself an ill-defined expression easily confounded with possession), in the latter as signifying those indefinite residual rights over things after all definite rights have been apportioned. In this sense property is one of the most beautiful and valuable technical terms in the jurist's vocabulary, and I should be sorry to blunt the edge of so admirable a tool; only I am quite at a loss for an English word to convey the idea of that particular right over a thing which gives him in whom that right is vested a similar right over the profits or fruits of any production of which the said thing may constitute one of the elements. It is strictly and invariably in this sense that I use the term *property;* and inasmuch as in most cases this right does form one of the residual indefinite rights referred to, I hope I may be pardoned for extending the use of the term for the sake of uniformity to those few cases in which it does not. The case of a free labourer working for wage is one of these. The fruits of his toil belong to his employer, although the residual indefinite rights over his own body are vested in himself. As I have explained, the plutologist will find it useful to regard the labourer as *pro tem.* the property of his employer—a slave let out on hire. If to the hypercritical sentimentalist this looks rather shocking, let him turn to the essay at the end of this volume and note the application of plutology to the solution of the labour question.

## CHAPTER VI.

### ANALYSIS.

In bringing to light a new science one is compelled to employ many terms before the right time has arrived for defining them, and to anticipate many truths of which the reader cannot be convinced until later in the work. Plutology forms no exception to this rule. I have already spoken of elements, of compounds, of profits, &c., and in the last chapter I was fain even to forestal vaguely what it is now time to explain fully. I there pointed out that "in all calculations of the cost of production of articles created with the assistance of labourers, the labourers themselves are invariably left out of the reckoning, and the cost of food, &c., required for their support alone considered."

This is a case of imperfect analysis. Now, if one rule is more important than all others in chemistry and plutology alike, it is the rule that analysis, to be worth anything, must be successive. We must patiently perform every one of a numerous series of successive analyses in the order of their synthesis, instead of rushing at once to the decomposition of our compound into its ultimate elements. Here is a statement which, if made in a work on chemistry, would raise a laugh from its obviousness, but if made in a work on political economy the laugh would probably be due to its novelty and absurd severity.

What would be thought of a chemist who should write cyanic ether in terms of its ultimate elements thus:—

$$C_3H_5NO, \text{ instead of } C\ (C_2H_5)\ NO, \text{ or } N \begin{cases} CO \\ C_2H_5 \end{cases};$$

or in some way which should show that one of the proximate elements is ether, $C_2H_5$? Or, to take another chemical illustration. Most of us are familiar with the taste of rancid butter; we are equally (it is to be hoped) familiar with the aroma of ripe apples, so noticeable in the flavour of good Devonshire cider. Analyse these two substances at once into their ultimate elements, and, strange to say, they are found to contain, not only the same substances, but precisely the same proportions of them. In fact, when once decomposed into their ultimate elements, no difference whatever exists between them; but that they are very different substances their successive analysis will show. Their proximate elements are quite different, and the steps of their synthesis are different.

Still, although the ultimate analysis of a compound is nothing like so complete or useful as successive analyses, it is not altogether worthless and misleading; there is, however, a third alternative which is infinitely worse. Let a chemist, for example, be required to analyse a bit of granite. Suppose that, instead of flying to the ultimate elements on the one hand, or the proximate on the other, he gave some in terms of the one and some in terms of the other.

Instead of oxygen, silicon, iron, calcium, &c., or of quartz, felspar, mica, &c., suppose he gave quartz, felspar, oxygen, iron, calcium, &c., what should we think of his analysis? or who would go to a chemist who described carbonate of ammonia as a compound of nitrogen, hydrogen, carbonic acid, and water? For Heaven's sake, we should say, leave the ammonia alone, or else split up your carbonic acid; let us have either proximate elements or ultimate, and not a jumble of the two. And yet this instance parallels, without the slightest exaggeration, the specimens of analysis afforded us by political economists. They always adopt this happy middle course, giving us some of the ingredients in their elementary form, and others in a high degree of complexity. You wish for a brick wall. You pay so much for bricks, so much for lime, so much for the use of vehicles of transport, and so much for the use of bricklayers. These are, roughly, the elements of the production. No one denies that what you have spent on the bricks is an element in the cost of the wall, no matter whether they are or are not at a monopoly price; and so with all the other elements till you come to the bricklayers. You are then informed that it is no longer a question of the market value of the commodity, viz.—bricklayers; it is a question merely of what the value might have been if the cost of supporting the bricklayers during the operation were alone taken into consideration. "Finally," writes Mill, "that large portion of the productive capital of the country which is employed in paying the wages and salaries of labourers is not all of it strictly indispensably necessary for production. Such of it as exceeds the actual necessaries of life and health (an excess which in the case of skilled labourers is usually considerable) is not expended in supporting labour, but in remunerating it." From which we are bidden to conclude " that whatever is so paid is not really applied to production, but to the unproductive consumption of productive labourers." Here is an engine hired by you to thrash your corn. Shall we say, then, that whatever you pay for the use of the engine in excess of what is necessary to supply it with fuel and to keep it in proper repair is not really applied to production, is not expended in supporting the engine, but in remunerating it? So stated the question appears ridiculous.

This inconsistency is clearly due to disregard of the principle of successive analysis. The proximate elements of the wall are, roughly as I have said, bricks, lime, vehicles, and bricklayers; but the political economists enumerate them thus: bricks, lime, vehicles, and (not labourers, but some of the elements of labourers—viz.) the necessaries of life and health required by the labourers during the process.

Why not at the same time enumerate the proximate elements of the bricks and lime—viz., clay, limestone, kilns, labourers, coals, sand, spades, and other tools; or why stop there? Why not analyse the kilns and the spades? In fine, as we said to the chemist who analysed carbonate of ammonia partly into proximate, partly into ultimate elements, "Give us all in terms of the one or in terms of the other, but for the sake of order and consistency don't jumble the two together."

Such a course not only produces disorder and confusion of thought, but, what is a most natural result, also leads to gross omissions. In the present instance it has led to an oversight which lies at the roots of all the absurd doctrines of capital and wages that have been built up by the economists. The value of the labourer himself is left out of the reckoning, his mere support for the time alone being considered. Unfortunately an enormous proportion of his wages goes, *not* to his temporary support, but to recoup the outlay on his production, such as he is. The disproportion exceeds all bounds as we rise in the scale of skilled labourers, till, when we reach the higher professions, the engineer with his twenty thousand a year expends so infinitesimal a fraction of his remuneration on his bare subsistence, that the economists have been driven to draw a hard and fast line between manual and other kinds of labourers—a most arbitrary one.

This new distinction is itself prolific of errors, and the whole story well bears out the ancient observation that one blunder leads to a hundred.

Next in importance to successive analysis—that is, the decomposition of the cost of an article in the order as nearly as possible of its synthesis—comes quantitative analysis. No chemist would be satisfied by being told that a certain substance is a compound of carbon, hydrogen, and chlorine. He might guess, but he certainly would not know, that it was chloroform. But as soon as he learns that the respective proportions of the component elements are as 1 : 1 : 3, he recognises it at once. If you describe a substance as a compound of carbon, oxygen, and hydrogen, he is still more at a loss. This time there is no guessing. Hundreds of organic acids, of ethers, alcohols, and what not, float before his mind's eye, and not till the mystic numbers are divulged has he the faintest conception of what substance you are speaking. The part these elements play in chemistry is paralleled by that played by labourers in plutology. They enter into a very large majority of all existing compounds, and it therefore behoves us to be more accurate in our quantitative calculations with these than with the others even.

In our analysis of a brick wall we must not only enumerate the bricks, lime, vehicles, and bricklayers, but we must set down the cost of each, otherwise our analysis is almost useless.

Having done this we may then safely proceed with the decomposition of these proximate elements themselves. In order to do this we transport ourselves to the fields of their respective creation—the lime-kilns, the brick-fields, the cartwright's, and the bricklayer's homes.

At the first we witness the kilns, the coals, the tools, the labourers, and the broad land on which the works stand. The cost of these we set down, and prove that we have omitted no important factor by comparing the sum of them with the price of the lime when ready for sale. Whether I have passed any of note we shall see in a future chapter.

On the brick-fields we see labourers again with wooden spades digging clay, others moulding it into grey bricks (now-a-days often done by machinery); there, again, are coals for burning the bricks, &c., &c.

At the cartwright's we see wrought-iron bars, and tires, and planks of wood, also labourers and tools, such as nails, and hammers, and saws, &c., paints and brushes, &c.

All these and the cost of them we set down and compare with the price of the barrows and carts.

But far more difficult is the analysis of the bricklayer. To perform this correctly we must learn the story of many lives and strike averages of expenses. It is far more easy to convert a joiner into a painter than it is to convert a sewing-machine into a pump.

And so it befalls that many men manufactured for one purpose are eventually utilised for another. But on an average the items of cost in the production of a joiner, or bricklayer, or plumber are discoverable to a very fine degree of approximation. A plumber costs the most of the three, and a joiner the next. As I have said, a large part of a bricklayer's remuneration goes to keep him in repair and at work; the rest goes to pay for the twelve years or so of his early life, his food and clothing and his education during his apprenticeship while he is learning his craft, also the rent of his lodgings, &c.

Subsequent to this comes the analysis of the cost of his usual food—wheaten bread, roast meat, potatoes, and beer; also of his clothing—corduroy coat, leather boots, worsted socks, &c.

Perhaps, though the limits of this short work do not permit of any analyses being performed in full, a fairly exhaustive one for illustration's sake may not be out of place. I will, therefore, endeavour to lay before the reader a trustworthy, if not altogether complete, analysis of a serge suit of clothes, value £5 4s. 2d., bought of a West-end tailor. I select this article because it is one in which all of us are more or less personally interested. All the information to be found in works on political economy on this and similar points consists in the statement that part of the purchase-money goes to reward the tailor in the shape of profits, part for raw material, part for the rent of the establishments in which it is manufactured and sold, and the rest in the wages of the labourers employed in the manufacturing processes.

Sometimes a bold spirit will point as far back as to the rent paid by the sheep-farmer who produces the raw wool, but this is done only incidentally and vaguely. There is nothing in it of the accurate, the complete, the scientific. In the following analysis each step will correspond with a separate process in the synthesis, or as nearly so as is necessary for the present purpose.

We must begin with the tailor. He receives five pounds four shillings and twopence (a very ordinary price) for the serge suit (not broadcloth, be it remembered, which is quite a different material from the goods manufactured out of the long wools now under analysis). I select this precise sum because it happens to contain exactly ten thousand half-farthings, and the fractions are easily expressed, therefore, in decimals. If we traced each of these smallest of English coins home to its source we might consider our dissection sufficiently exhaustive; but this I shall not here attempt to do. I shall stop short in the case of most of them long before reaching this point; and others, again, I shall follow further.

First of all the tailor gives eleven shillings a yard for a good serge, such as suits are made of for India. In most cases he purchases it of the cloth-merchant, as he is called in the North, or draper, or mercer, as Londoners style him. The latter charges a small percentage for his risk in wholesale speculation, for warehousing, and for carriage from the manufacturer's in the North to the London market. Frequently, however, West-end tailors buy direct from the manufacturer, and as the carriage and warehousing of the cloth constitute a very minute fraction in the cost of our suit, I propose to disregard the cloth-merchant altogether. It takes about three yards and a-half of serge to make a suit. This, at eleven shillings a yard, is £1 18s 6d., or little more than a third of the cost of the suit. Linings, canvas, paddings, thread, buttons, &c., devour another ten shillings and sixpence. Braid comes to about four and fivepence, bringing up the total sum paid for materials to £2 13s. 5d., or about half the cost of the suit. Next comes the rent of the shop, on which some West-end tailors and other tradesmen build so much in defending themselves against the charge of overcharging. This formidable item absorbs about sevenpence of the £5 4s. 2d., sometimes less, and occasionally a trifle more. Next come the labourers—namely, the journeymen tailors and shopmen. Their wages at a first-rate establishment, where good work is exacted, could not amount to less than about £1 14s., including extras, leaving sixteen and twopence for superintendence (usually undertaken by the proprietor himself in the plutological sense) and for real profits. Such are the proximate elements of our suit of serge. I shall dismiss them all with the single exception of the stuff itself, price £1 18s. 6d., as it was bought of the manufacturer.

We have now reached the threshold of the manufacture of the cloth itself, and here the analysis becomes very interesting. The processes through which the wool passes on its way from the sheep's back to our own are very numerous, and more or less differentiated. In some mills all these processes are carried on under the same roof (*i.e.*, from the *sorting* to the *finishing*), but this is not the general rule; and even if the exceptions were in the minority, the plutologist would take advantage of such exceptions to render his analysis more complete because more gradual.

However, the minor processes are invariably performed by the same firm, and it is, therefore, impossible to make more than three stages in our descent from the finished cloth to the fleece as received from the wool-broker. These three stages correspond to the weaving and its subsidiary processes, the spinning and its subsidiary processes, and the combing and its subsidiary processes. Now the weaving, spinning, and combing being all carried on in large sheds by means of complicated machinery and organised armies of skilled workpeople, resemble one another sufficiently to render a detailed analysis of each of them both tedious, and, for our present purpose, superfluous. Of course in a technical work written for the express benefit of trade such a detailed analysis of every department would be absolutely essential to its usefulness, but here it is otherwise.

I shall, therefore, pass over the first two (in order of analysis, the last two in order of time) of these— namely, the weaving and spinning—and proceed at once to the consideration of the combing. In the meantime our material has dwindled down in cost from £1 18s. 6d., at which it was sold to the cloth-merchant, to five shillings and sixpence, at which it is sold by the comber to the spinner ready to be spun. The spinners and weavers have, therefore, absorbed no less than £1 13s. 0d. Serge is a twill of worsted warp and woollen weft. The comber, inasmuch as he combs both long wools and short, is the precursor of both the woollen-cloth manufacturer and the worsted manufacturer, and he performs, amongst others of less importance, the following processes: sorting, or separating the fleece as it comes to him in bales, into kinds; scouring, devilling, picking, oiling, scribbling, carding, and combing; and if the required article is to be wool-dyed instead of piece-dyed, he performs the dying also.

For these purposes large sheds are built within easy access of railways, with an accessible supply of cheap water and in the neighbourhood of skilled labourers. These three pre-requisites have drawn the combing business of this country into the West Riding of Yorkshire, and especially to Bradford; and since combing must be carried on on a very large scale in order to be commercially profitable, while it is at the same time subject to considerable fluctuations, the competition in the trade is small, and very large profits are realised. This accounts for the large item set down in the following analysis to comber's profits.

The sheds are full of machinery of many different kinds, the chief of which are the washing and back-washing machines, the carding engines, the combing machines, and the engine that works the whole. Each machine is superintended by one or two men or women, who are themselves looked after by a foreman of the department, who receives a high salary from the master or company as the case may be. Another group of men of superior status to the other mill-hands is to be found in the sorting-room, separating the fleece into *picklocks*, *choice*, *seconds*, *fine abb*, *livery*, &c., while others mind the engine and others the books in the office. In order that the reader may verify my figures, I shall first furnish him with a fair account of the outlay required on such a shed as I have described, of the particulars of the expenses incurred in keeping it up, in paying the wages and salaries of those employed, and of the gross receipts of the undertaking.

In the first place, the price of the raw wool as it is bought at the London wool-sales varies considerably according to its quality, some sorts being obtainable at eightpence and others at two shillings a pound, and the majority at intermediate prices, averaging about eighteenpence per pound.

A moderate-sized shed, properly fitted up at a total outlay of about £76,000, would, if fully employed, comb about 7,700lbs. of wool per day, or 2,310,000lbs. per year of 300 days. The cost of combing the different classes of wools also varies considerably, some kinds costing more than double what other kinds do. We may, however, strike the average at fourpence per pound. Consequently, the wool which was bought for £173,250 would be sold again, combed and ready to be spun, for £211,750, leaving us a balance to account for of £38,500.

As I have before said, the comber's net profits must be set down at a considerable percentage on his outlay, for reasons which I have given. Fifteen, seventeen, and even twenty per cent. is not uncommon in good years. Twelve and a-half is a fair estimate; and this on an outlay of £76,000 is £9,500. This sum represents the comber's profits, and deducting it from the £38,500 we have still to account for £29,000.

Now the elements of production, as we have seen, divide themselves into two classes—those which are essentially consumed and those which are accidentally consumed, and among the latter we find the sheds, the engines, and machinery, and shafting, &c., which, inasmuch as they endure for many years, do not require to be paid for except by instalments. Seven and a-half per cent. is a reasonable deduction for this purpose, although ten per cent. is usually taken. This gives £5,700 for wear and tear and use of so-called fixed capital. All the labourers together, including managers, foremen, mill-hands male and female, and clerks, would absorb about £9,700, while the coals, soap, and oil would cost respectively £3,000, £4,500, and £3,000, or thereabouts, leaving some £3,100 for gas, carriage, packing, stamps, taxes, &c., &c., &c.

Nothing now remains to be done but to perform the very simple operation of expressing the ratios which these figures bear to one another in fractions of 5s. 6d., the price paid for the portion of serge required to make one suit of clothes.

Clearly, we have 4s. 6d. for raw material—that is, the fleece or wool in the grease. The remaining shilling must be divided amongst the comber, his *employés*, the mill and machinery (accidentally-consumed capital), the coals, the soap, and the oil (essentially consumed capital), and sundries (both one and the other). Let us arrange them in the form of a table.

| | | | | | |
|---|---|---|---|---|---|
| Comber | $\frac{95}{385}$ | of a shilling, or | nearly 2d. | | $\frac{31}{32}$ |
| Plant | $\frac{57}{385}$ | ,, | ,, | 1d. | $\frac{25}{32}$ |
| Wages | $\frac{97}{385}$ | ,, | ,, | ·3d. | $\frac{1}{32}$ |
| Coals | $\frac{30}{385}$ | ,, | ,, | | $\frac{30}{32}$ |
| Soap | $\frac{45}{385}$ | ,, | ,, | 1d. | $\frac{13}{32}$ |
| Oil | $\frac{30}{385}$ | ,, | ,, | | $\frac{30}{32}$ |
| Sundries | $\frac{31}{385}$ | ,, | ,, | | $\frac{31}{32}$ |
| | | | | | 12d. |

Here we see that the comber receives about threepence for his services in combing the wool for our suit of clothes, while all the various kinds of subordinate labourers receive among them about the same sum or a trifle (half a farthing) more. The oil, regarded as so expensive an element in the cost of manufacturing woollen goods, turns out to absorb less than one penny of the £5 4s. 2d. given for our suit, while the use of all that beautiful and intricate machinery costs us less than twopence.

This analysis does not profess to be anything like an exhaustive one; in that case we should have to follow up the soap through its preparation to its origin, also the oil and the coals. I will only take two of the items, however—the labourers and machinery—as it will be interesting to ascertain the exact sum received by those oily mill-girls that one meets in Hunslet, shawl on head on week-days, and so gaudily decked out in all the colours of the rainbow on Sundays, for their contribution in toil to the manufacture of the clothes we wear.

Such a shed as the one above described would contain about two hundred women employed in the combing, gilling, carding, and backwashing, receiving about half-a-crown a day each. The men employed receive sums varying considerably, from the foreman at about £350 a year to the porters at £45, and cleaners at even less. A dozen men at the washing machines at 4s. a day, ten at repairs and the engine at 5s. a day, a dozen overlookers at 7s. a day, three bookkeepers at different salaries varying from £120 to £60 per annum, three porters at 3s. a day, several doorkeepers, cleaners, &c., at various wages, and a foreman at £300 a year. Let us arrange these in the form of a table, reckoned at so much a day :—

|  |  |  |  |  |  | £ | s. | d. |
|---|---|---|---|---|---|---|---|---|
| Women | Carding | 80 | } at 2s. per day | = | 20 | 0 | 0 |
|  | Gilling | 70 |  |  |  |  |  |
|  | Combing | 40 |  |  |  |  |  |
|  | Backwashing | 10 |  |  |  |  |  |
| Men | Washing | 12 | at 4s. | ,, | = | 2 | 8 | 0 |
|  | Mechanics | 10 | ,, 5s. | ,, | = | 2 | 10 | 0 |
|  | Overlookers | 12 | ,, 7s. | ,, | = | 4 | 4 | 0 |
|  | Bookkeepers | 3 |  |  |  | 1 | 0 | 0 |
|  | Foreman | 1 |  |  |  | 1 | 0 | 0 |
|  | Porters | 3 | ,, 3s. |  |  | 0 | 9 | 0 |
|  | Doorkeepers, cleaners &c. |  |  |  | 0 | 15 | 8 |
|  |  |  |  |  |  | £32 | 6 | 8 |

All these figures added together yield us £32 6s. 8d., and if we multiply this sum by 300 for the number of working days in the year, we have £9,700 per annum, the amount, as will be remembered, which was set down for the labourers in the cost of combing.

Thus it appears nearly twice as much is paid in this department of manufacture to women than to men, though their average receipts are, of course, much smaller.

Of the women employed about forty attend to the combing machines, and they may, therefore, be regarded as the combers or combresses (according to our grammatical proclivities) *par excellence*. Hence we may affirm that these young ladies (as they style one another) receive no less than $\frac{1}{8}$ of all that is spent on the labour-element consumed in combing the wool used in the suit of clothes. In good round coin of the realm, then, this amounts to an eighth of threepence, or thereabouts—THREE HALF-FARTHINGS!

If ever you complain to your tailor about his excessive charge for your last serge suit, remember you are open to the retort, "Well, sir, if you will go to

Bradford and undertake the combing of the wool required for your next suit yourself, we shall be happy to deduct three half-farthings from our charge; and furthermore, if you will purchase your own fleece, sort it, wash it, oil it, card it, comb it, and deliver it to the spinner ready to be spun, we can afford to let you have the five-guinea suit for five pounds."

Perhaps a detailed analysis of the £5,700 set down to wear and tear and use of mill, engines and machinery, would now become tedious. I will, therefore, merely remark that about $\frac{1}{6}$ would go for the mill itself, without shafting or fittings, about $\frac{1}{25}$ for shafting and straps, $\frac{1}{5}$ for carding engines, $\frac{1}{6}$ for combing machines, and $\frac{1}{15}$ for engine and boilers, $\frac{1}{4}$ for backwashing machines with gills, and the rest in card-clothing, gills, tools, &c., &c. Go and see one of these, say the huge engine itself at work, and examine its details, and remember that this beautiful and wonderful structure must also be traced back to its source in the iron-beds and coal-fields before our suit of clothes can be said to have found its pedigree. One-fifteenth of a penny-three-farthings, or rather less than half a farthing, repays the engine and boilers that work the combing machinery that combs the fleece that forms the yarn that is warp and woof in the clothes we wear.

I should like to have conducted the reader as far at least as the sheep on the South Downs, or on the Australian sheep-farm, before quitting it, but I fear many will already either complain of the length to which I have gone, or skip the chapter altogether. To me the subject is absorbing because of its immense importance. Before very long I sincerely hope those who are more competent than I will take it up, and each in his own branch of manufacture, or of trade, present us with a complete analysis of every article of wealth around us. When once certain kinds of wealth have been fairly analysed every succeeding analysis will become easier and easier. Coals, for instance, enter into the composition of almost every article which is manufactured in a greater or smaller amount; iron does the same in the form of machinery and other tools. Labourers, too, are many of them brought up on similar food and at a like expense, and an analysis of several kinds of them will serve for a very large number.

The advantage of converting the original £5 4s. 2d. into 10,000 half-farthings enables us to present the analyses in the form of a table in which all the fractions are expressed in decimals, for the use of those who prefer to regard them as percentages of the whole:—

| Suit 10,000 | Cloth 3696 Tailor 1552 Wages 3264 Rent 56 Linings, &c. 1008 Braid 424 | *Tailoring process.* | Cloth 3512 Merchant Wages Rent Carriage, &c. | *Cloth-retailing process.* | Yarn Weaver Wages Rent Machinery Coals Sundries | *Weaving, &c., process.* | Wool 528 Spinner Wages Rent Machinery Coals &c. | *Spinning, &c., process.* | Raw wool 432 Comber 23·75 Wages 24 Rent 1·0 Machinery 13·25 Coals 7·5 Oil 7·5 Soap 11·25 Sundries 7·75 | *Combing, &c., process.* | Raw wool Broker Wages Rent Shipping &c. | *Shipping, &c., process.* | | *Sheep-farming process.* |
|---|---|---|---|---|---|---|---|---|---|---|---|---|---|
| Total | 10,000 | | 3696 | | 3512 | | | | 528 | | 432 | | |

The reader may himself supply all the other figures, and he will find not only that it is an excellent exercise, but that it is one which cannot be effected without inquiries at the seats of the respective processes. Books are silent on the subject. Tables of analysis would not, as a rule, require to do more than follow up what is called the raw material to its source, as is done in the above table. To follow up the other elements would render the table unwieldy and confusing, and, besides, a book of analyses would be certain to contain the majority of them in separate tables. Having once traced a certain percentage of the whole to coals (say) a figure could point out the page where the analysis of coal is to be found, and that would suffice.

Another observation is to be made with respect to the above specimen table, to the effect that it is quite optional to what degree of particularity we conduct our analysis, provided only that we keep apart the separate processes or steps in the synthesis; for example, we may, in the analysis of the combing-process, simply enumerate, as I have done, the wool, the comber, the labourers, the plant, the coal, the oil, the soap, and sundries, or we may specify the kinds of many of these general classes thus: raw wool, comber, washing-men, sorters, gilling, carding, combing, and backwashing-women, mechanics, overlookers, bookkeepers, foreman, porters, doorkeepers, &c., mill, rent of land, engine and boilers, carding-engines, combing-machines, backwashing-machines, card-clothing, gills, tools, &c., coal, soap, oil, gas, water, taxes, carriage, package, &c. It is merely a question of precision *versus* simplicity, and our choice must depend upon the object we have in view.

Of one thing, however, we must be careful—not to confound enumeration with analysis. We do not analyse machinery into engine, combing machines, &c.; we merely enter into details and avoid hasty classification.

But of this more anon.

Let me again, before closing this chapter, recall the fact that all the materials for a complete book of analytical tables are at hand, and require only to be digested. Never, in my opinion, was so great a desideratum so easy of attainment, requiring only the co-operation of a number of traders and manufacturers superintended and co-ordinated as to their efforts and results by a single compiler not averse to simple arithmetical calculations. Surely this public benefit will not have long to wait for public benefactors.

## CHAPTER VII.

### ON SOME PROMINENT ELEMENTS.

I BELIEVE that the chief if not the only explanation to account for the absence of such tables as those described in the foregoing chapter is to be found in the prevalent theories of capital and labour and their resulting confusions and stultifications.

The present chapter will be devoted to the special consideration of certain prominent elements in production.

The first remark which a study of several such analyses calls forth has reference to the enormous proportion which this labourer-element bears to all others. At every turn we are met not only with this element but with a very considerable amount of it (measured in value). Superficial observation has resulted in a similar discovery, leading, as is usual with unscientific and inaccurate persons, to the hasty and false generalisation embodied in the doctrine that every commodity owes whatever of value it possesses entirely to labour. This doctrine has been embraced by the large majority of great political economists, and, like most of their doctrines, it is not only untrue, but, even when nearest the truth, perfectly barren of result. What if it did turn out, as they would have us believe, that the streets of London owe the whole of their value as sites to the labour that has been expended on them? I fail to see any scientific laws to be deduced from such a theory. It is, however, fair to admit that the immense preponderance of the labourer-element in all *ultimate* analyses does afford some justification of the error. I say *ultimate* because, in proximate analyses this element is not, as a rule, so very disproportionate to the rest, or even the greatest.

The ratio which the ultimate labourer-element bears to the other ultimate elements has frequently been made the basis of classification otherwise described. The difference between a commodity containing a large proportion of that element and a commodity containing a small proportion is, of course, merely a difference of degree, like the difference between a strong and a weak solution of salt.

The ratio is small in a ruby ring, larger in a sack of coals, larger still in a loaf of bread, and largest of all in a grand pianoforte. The distinction is of importance only in so far as it affects the demand for labourers.

Another observation called forth by the study of these analyses is the vast variety in kind and value of labourers themselves. By labourers I mean throughout this work all valuable human beings, and such human beings in so far only as they are valuable. I include the manager as well as the errand-boy, the actress as well as the bootmaker.

Now it will be noticed that I separated the labourers in my analysis of the several cloth-manufacturing processes from the cloth-merchant, the tailor, the spinner, the comber, &c. I did this for the sake of simplicity, and because I was justified in doing it by a certain considerable minority of cases in which the latter persons do no work whatever in superintending or otherwise, relegating the functions of management entirely to some other person whom I have purposely confounded with the foreman. As a fact, most tailors and all cloth-merchants work themselves either by superintendence or manual labour, while, in the manufacturing processes, the heads of the establishments or proprietors of the elements are frequently wholly idle, like the landlord in the agricultural process.

In this case their reward bears no proportion whatever to their value, but to the increased value of the produce—the difference between the value of the compound and that of the sum of all the elements.

Whenever the proprietor of the elements likewise works in any way his reward must be divided into two parts—the one must be regarded as the value of his services, and the other as the increment of value due to the combination. In the capacity of worker or manager he is classed with the labourers—that is, in those cases in which it is sufficient to class them together at all, instead of specifying the various kinds, as should be done almost always.

There is one class of labourer to whom attention must be especially drawn. It is one thing to manage a going concern, and quite another to start a new industry, to conceive the expediency of performing certain combinations hitherto unexperimented upon, though both are performed by the same kind of labourer. This man, so notorious as the promoter of bubble companies, is nevertheless, in his less conspicuous capacity of an honest schemer in trades and manufactures, one of the most praiseworthy and valuable contributors to production. The general name of that class of labourers whose function it is to conceive and carry out the idea, to perform the calculation demonstrating the profitableness of the scheme, is not easy to decide upon. The best is, perhaps, that of combiner; and yet this is objectionable, as seeming to imply that he does not himself, like other labourers, enter into the combination. On the contrary, however, he not only enters into the combination, but is a most valuable ingredient thereof, as is proved by the high remuneration he receives for his services.

For example, here is a young man innocent of business but anxious to invest £20,000 at 10 per cent. A man without other visible property than his own body steps forward and produces references as to his abilities and experience, and forthwith a partnership is entered into according to the articles of which the two partners receive equal moieties of the profits of the undertaking. In this frequently-occurring case the combiner clearly values himself at £20,000, and his annual services at £2,000, more or less, according to the risk of the undertaking in which he is experienced. If the business is not only a new but a novel one, it is clearly a risky one, dependent as it is for success on the accuracy of the combiner's reckonings; if it is a new one on a well-known model it is less so; while if it is an old-established going concern the combiner is but a manager or managing partner, and the risk is still less. Again, let it be remembered, if the proprietor is his own combiner, his reward must be regarded as coming through two distinct channels—proprietor's profits and combiner's value.

Next to labourers, some of the most common, and at the same time least regarded, elements of production are those which may be classed together under the general name of transport-elements.

Before we can say that such is the price or value of any commodity we must first ascertain where that commodity happens to be. On the banks of the Thames oranges are worth about a penny each, on the banks of the Amazon next to nothing at all.

Coal at the bottom of the pit is worth less than at the pit's mouth, and less at the pit's mouth than on a London wharf. Timber has no value in parts of Canada or Brazil, while it is very costly in England. Most manufactured textile fabrics and iron goods are cheaper in England than in India, and, without multiplying examples, it is obvious that the element of transport has much to do with this disparity of values in different localities. In cases of this kind, when the difference between the values of the same commodity in different places is greater than the cost of transporting it from the one to the other, the transportation takes place, and the difference is readjusted so as to exactly equal the cost of the transport. But when the difference is less than enough to defray the expenses of carriage, no such transportation takes place.

In speaking of the value of any article we must always be understood to mean at the nearest market, unless the contrary is stated. The statement that sound new port is worth less than sixpence a quart, though true at Oporto, is misleading to the English reader, unless the locality is mentioned.

Now transport, though a useful general term, is no metaphysical notion. Like all other elements of which I take note, it denotes solid material substances —ships, flesh and blood, iron engines, coals, &c.

Let there be no misunderstanding on this score. Plutology admits of no immaterialities.

Most articles of value can be transported from one locality to another with profit. Corn, coals, manufactured goods, even cattle and meats, are continually travelling from place to place—from where they are cheap to where they are dear. There are, however, some commodities which cannot be so conveyed with advantage. Valuable as is a good soil in Middlesex, and valueless and abundant as it is in Central Africa, still it will not pay to convey it from one place to the other.

In Flanders, no doubt, soil has been carted from fertile to barren spots at a remunerative outlay, but as a rule it cannot be done.

This brings us to the consideration of a third important and common element of production. It is land. This term is used by political economists to denote and to confound two distinct and very different commodities, the one a chemical substance, depending for its value on its chemical constituents and the proportions of them, and also, like everything else, upon its locality; the other depending for its value upon its locality only, having no other usefulness than that of affording standing room. The first of these is soil, and the second is ground. (Land is already too ambiguous for the present explanation.) The value of soil depends upon the thickness of the layer of it on the ground, and upon its texture and chemical composition, both of which are continually undergoing alterations at the hands of the agriculturist. It is too bulky to be worth removal, and when removed would require spreading over a considerable surface of ground to render it productive of corn, &c. Moreover, ground in some parts cannot be more profitably employed than in combination with the soil which happens to lie on its surface. This accounts for the fact that they are *usually* sold together, and, as a consequence, confounded together by the economists. But though usually they are not always sold together. Frequently the ground is found to be more valuable for other purposes than to have soil spread over it, even though the soil be ready spread, in which case the soil is sometimes taken off and sold at a low price, or simply neglected, or given away as not worth more than carriage. In these cases the ground is made use of for roads, for canals, for buildings, for piazzas, for drill-grounds, for skating-rinks, playgrounds, &c., &c.

It has been said that soil is cumbrous to move, and, therefore, seldom moved. Sometimes, however, it is conveyed from place to place, and in certain forms certainly, its elements are transported like all other manufactures. I refer to the permanent and organic manures. What I wish to notice is that soil *can* be transported. Ground, on the contrary, cannot. Overlying waters may be drained off, or *terra firma* may be created, so to speak, by building piers and the like on submerged ground, but all this does not affect the truth of the statement that ground *cannot* be transported.

This very simple fact has given rise to one of the most singular doctrines of which political economy can boast, and their name is Legion. Let me state it in the exact words of its inculcators. "Land is not an element in the cost of agricultural production." Buckle admits that only the initiated can clearly perceive this truth. Let us hope that one usually so lucid himself felt a little misty about this economical paradox. Mr. Fawcett, however, being Professor of Political Economy at the University of Cambridge, has pondered long over its mysteries, and he pronounces himself competent to make this doctrine plain even to ordinary capacities. I confess it is not yet brought down to my comprehension.

"Let us now suppose," he writes, "that all land is made rent-free by an arbitrary edict of the Government. Such a spoliation, although it would unjustly interfere with the rights of property, would not cause any diminution in the consumption of food. The same quantity of agricultural produce would be required as before. The same area of land would, therefore, have to be cultivated. That land would still require to be tilled which previously only paid a nominal rent. But if food were rendered cheaper by making land rent-free, the land which before only paid a nominal rent would be cultivated at a loss. No person, however, will continue to apply his labour to capital if he does not obtain in return the ordinary rate of profit; and, therefore, if food became cheaper, such land as we have just described would cease to be cultivated. But this cannot be, because the demand of the country for food is such that the produce which the land yields cannot be dispensed with. It is, therefore, manifest that food would not become cheaper even if land were made rent-free. Rent, consequently, is not an element in the cost of production."

Now the whole of this paragraph is sound, logical, and clear, with the exception of the last sentence, which educes a consequent by no means involved in the premises. To begin with, land could not by any possibility be made rent-free, either by an arbitrary edict of Government or in any other way. There are two ways, or more, in which such a thing might be *attempted.* Farmers might be protected by the State against the demands of landlords; but this would be merely to remove the rent from the pockets of the landlords into that of farmers for the time being. The edict would simply amount in the end to compelling all landowners to farm their own land.

The other plausible mode of attempting to effect the same result would be by taxing the landlords to the full extent of their rent. This, it is obvious, is only another way of dividing the rent amongst the whole population, or of what is advocated under the title of vesting all the land of the country in the State. The State becomes the landlord, and the farmers pay the same rent as they did under private landlords.

The bare supposition that the value of land could possibly be annihilated is absurd. The only circumstance which could bring about such a result would be the previous cessation of the demand for corn and agricultural produce generally. This is tantamount to the annihilation of the population; and hence the depopulation of the country is the necessary condition of rent-free land. By supposing impossibilities and absurdities we may demonstrate anything, even to ordinary intellects.

Let us make a parallel supposition. Let us suppose that shippers and brokers, and all other persons interested in the remuneration paid for the transportation of corn, were unexpectedly taxed to the full amount of their gains. Would food be cheaper? Certainly not. May we then conclude that ships, railways, &c., are not elements in the cost of production? Or suppose the owners of coal-fields were informed that henceforth they would receive nothing for their coals, would that bring about a reduction in all commodities requiring coal for their manufacture? Certainly not. Those manufacturers of iron who required it would be driven to extract it themselves, and would pocket the proceeds instead of giving it to the consumer of their manufactures in the shape of reduced prices. Clearly the same reasons which induce coal-owners to sell less at a high price rather than more at a bare profit on the workings would have precisely the same weight with manufacturers; and if you contend that manufacturers could afford to spare large profits on the coal, because they would recoup themselves out of the extended sale of their own manufactures, I reply that, if this were so, coal-owners would undoubtedly turn manufacturers themselves. Upon this theory, so obvious to Mr. Fawcett, Mill has the following cautious remarks (*Principles*, Book III., c. iv.) :—

"Does rent enter into cost of production? And the answer of the best economists is in the negative. The temptation is strong to the adoption of these sweeping expressions, even by those who are aware of the restrictions with which they must be taken; for there is no denying that they stamp a general principle more firmly on the mind than if it were hedged round in theory with all its practical limitations. But they also puzzle and mislead, and create an impression unfavourable to political economy, as if it disregarded the evidence of facts. No one can deny that rent sometimes enters into cost of production. If I buy or rent a piece of ground and build a cloth-manufactory on it, the ground-rent forms legitimately a part of my expenses of production which must be repaid by the product. And since all factories are built on ground, and most of them in places where ground is peculiarly valuable, the rent paid for it must, on the average, be compensated in the values of all things made in factories." After this qualification Mill contends that rent is not an element in the cost of production which determines the value of *agricultural* produce. Let us see whether this is true. Let us make a supposition which is conceivable, and indeed probable, as a future fact. Suppose the value of fertile land (*i.e.*, ground with a thick layer of rich soil on the surface) to sink in value, owing to a diminished demand for it for park and pleasure-ground purposes. Would not this affect the value of corn? Undoubtedly it would. The newly-competing fertile soils would throw the barely-remunerative soils altogether out of the market. Lands which formerly paid no rent over and above farmers' profits would now cease to pay even the latter. The same quantity of corn would be produced, but less land would be employed for the purpose, and the cost of "that portion of the supply which is produced and brought to market at the greatest expense," and which, according to the law of value of Mill's third class of commodities (and as is admitted on all hands), regulates the value of all the rest, would be considerably lowered. Hence surely rent *is* an element in the cost of even agricultural production.

## CHAPTER VIII.

### SYNTHESIS.

IN considering the synthesis of plutological combinations we are of course considering the same phenomena as when we are occupied with the analysis, but in the reverse order. The order of time is that which we must now follow, so as to fix our attention upon the causes to which the several steps of the process are due.

We have already observed that commodities which might have been consumed in one way, perhaps immediately gratificable, are devoted to another purpose which eventually results in the creation of a more valuable if not a more enjoyable commodity. Why is this procrastination permitted by the proprietor? Because the new compound is expected to be more valuable. An increment of new value is looked forward to. But to what is this increment attributable? Why, after a certain combination or mixture of commodities, is the public ready to give more than for the commodities separately—that is, uncombined; and who decides what the extra charge shall be?

What do the political economists tell us? They say that this extra sum charged and acquiesced in by the purchaser is the reward of *saving*—"the wages of abstinence." Bear that in mind. Capital, say they unanimously, is the result of saving. Profits are the fair and natural reward for waiting—for saving. No doctrine is more incessantly harped on than this one. And yet it is false. Nothing whatever is paid for saving by any one to any one. Even interest is not paid for waiting, as will presently be shown.

I would insist on nothing more strongly than on the *growth* of wealth. Plutology deals in *fructifying causes*. Out of vegetables and soil, plus inorganic environment, spring by action, and reaction, and assimilation, *more* vegetables and *more* soil, plus inorganic environment. So out of men and wealth, plus useless environment, spring more men and more wealth, plus useless environment.

Wealth, in other words, is reproductive—it is fruitful and multiplies. Like leaven, it tends to leaven the lump. Otherwise how do we account for the fact that there is more wealth in the world to-day than there was a thousand years ago? Saving can at best only preserve the existing; it cannot increase the quantity.

Numerous compounds are doubtless made which are not more valuable, and others which are actually less valuable, than the sum of their ingredients, but the combiner who put them together expected a different result.

Experience teaches to avoid such combinations in future, and only those are persisted in which prove fruitful.

The new increment of value is called profit, and it belongs to the proprietor or proprietors of the original elements. All the ingredients contribute to the augmented value of the product in proportion to their respective values before the process. This is obvious, for, were it not so, the articles supposed to be more efficacious would be bought by the proprietor of the other ingredients first and mixed in afterwards. Their owner might refuse to sell at the usual prices, and the values would rise till there was no disputing that they contributed to the new value in proportion to their own original value as compared with the remaining elements.

Not only is saving incompetent to account for the increase of wealth, but it is actually never paid for at all. Does any one pay you for keeping loaves in your pantry or gold in your purse? Not a bit of it. If you keep port in your cellars for some years you certainly do receive a higher price for it than if you sold it at once. But then the article has undergone a real change. It is another article for which the value is higher. Not only is the rent to be recouped, but it is manifest that you have the fewer competitors in the manufacture, as I may call it, of old port, for the simple reason that the new port has a value which will fetch other commodities, which, by being judiciously combined, will increase in value at even a higher rate than your port will. But you are not paid for *saving*, else you would be paid also for saving anything else of equal value an equal time— grapes for example: try the experiment.

But it is urged if you lend a hundred pounds to a manufacturer for a year you will receive it back, and with it an additional five pounds; surely this is your reward for not spending it at once.

This brings us to the subject of interest, which some regard as a mystery.

Those of us who have enough to eat, and to wear, and to spare, are anxious, very naturally, not to *save*, but to *combine* our surplus, in order that when we have need of it we may find it increased in value. But it is one thing to be willing, and another thing to be able, to combine commodities profitably. They will, fortunately, however, combine themselves, provided one of the ingredients be a *combiner*. Hence we look out for a combiner, and with his advice procure by exchange the other requisite ingredients; or, what amounts to the same thing, we entrust our surplus wealth to him for combination.

As a consequence of this we are sometimes lucky and sometimes unlucky; sometimes our profits are large and sometimes small; and sometimes even nil or minus. On the average of all such transactions in this country we find that our profits amount to about three-hundredths of the outlay in one year. Consequently, if our investments are sufficiently numerous, we shall, without taking any trouble ourselves, receive, by the mere expedient of lending, about 3 per cent. on our investments. This average profit differs in different countries and in different periods; indeed, it is continually fluctuating. Perhaps we should be nearer the mark if we named $3\frac{1}{2}$ per cent. as the average increment in this country at present. One, therefore, who refuses to take any trouble, or to incur any risk, is entitled to expect 3 per cent. at least per annum as the average increment of value on any property which he may be willing to combine with other kinds. This average profit has received the name of *interest*. By some unaccountable confusion or other, interest has been accustomed to be regarded as something altogether different from profit, and as the reward of saving.

When the average annual profit on combinations sinks through the rashness or stupidity of combiners to less than $3\frac{1}{2}$ per cent., many proprietors not quite so thrifty as their neighbours prefer to consume their surplus wealth at once as luxuries or what not, rather than to invest them at so trumpery a remuneration. The supply of general commodities (other than combiners) is diminished, and their value rises again slightly in consequence to meet the demand, and the average reward is thereby prevented from falling below a certain level. In Holland it has been known to fall very far below $3\frac{1}{2}$ per cent. per annum, so we must give our Dutch neighbours credit for greater thrift than ourselves.

Whenever the element of *risk* enters into an investment the talent of the combiner is at once brought into play, and speculators on the Stock Exchange are of course combiners in the highest sense of the word. The combiner's function, as I have said, is this very one of calculating chances. So that if you are receiving more than some $3\frac{1}{2}$ per cent. per annum for your money, you may put down the difference to the account of your own services as a skilled labourer, but do not underscore the word "skilled" until time has proved that even if the principal were lost you have done better than if you had originally invested in land or Consols.

I have mentioned the rashness or stupidity of combiners as a cause of low average profits, and consequent diminished supply of general commodities for combination. The raised value of general commodities is only another expression for the lowered value of combiners, which is a most proper result of their inefficiency. Credit is said to be bad, because, forsooth, careful people will not entrust their wealth to combiners who have proved themselves incapable. When the proprietors of general commodities are willing to entrust them to combiners at a small remuneration—small, that is to say, according to the risky nature of the undertaking—credit is said to be good. Credit sometimes becomes so good, combiners are so highly esteemed and relied on, that even the most speculative and rash amongst them succeed in enticing proprietors to invest in their schemes. Companies for all sorts of wild and impracticable purposes are promoted, and the business of old going concerns receives a strong stimulus. But not for long. Soon the bubbles burst. Many proprietors of general commodities are ruined, and, warned by their example, their neighbours cease to wish to invest at small, or indeed at any, remuneration. What is called a commercial panic ensues. Manufacturers and traders—combiners generally—are regarded with extreme distrust, and, according to the kind of combination in which they are skilled, sink in value to an extent which compels them to lie idle till a more propitious season. Meantime many of them perish altogether, and others are converted into labourers of a more valuable kind for the period.

The exhaustive treatment of this branch of the subject will be of great value to commerce and to the legislature. The erroneous notions at present prevalent have led to the most extraordinary blunders, of which the Joint Stock Companies Acts are prominent examples; but as this work does not profess to deal with the applications of plutology, I shall reserve the consideration of partnerships to a future occasion.

Has the ordinary manufacturer very clear ideas of profit? In spite of their reputation for keenness and insight, I must confess that from the nature of many contracts that I have investigated, drawn up between men of ability and standing in business, I am led to the conclusion that their ideas are, as a rule, of the vaguest, and their success in practice seems to be due rather to instinct or habit than to reasoning.

To begin with, we hear of net profits and of gross profits. Sometimes we even hear of wages or salaries being paid out of profits. Frequently interest at 5 per cent. is deducted before stating the profits of the business, and so forth.

Let us take as complicated a case as we can find around us. Here is a firm consisting of a managing partner and a sleeping partner. They also have a foreman at a good salary, who helps the managing partner. The plant, including land, buildings, and machinery, is valued at £10,000. At the end of a single process occupying four months, on stock-taking, it is found that the whole property, plant and materials together, are worth £12,500. Now, £500 has already been paid in wages, and £1,000 in raw materials, coals, &c., making the total outlay £11,500.

The increment of new value at first sight appears to be £1,000, but of this the manager has to deduct one-third of his salary of £300 per annum. Thi reduces it to £900. But the managing partner is entitled to something for his exertions in superintending the business, and as he may be supposed to be both more careful and more intelligent than his foreman, let him take double the latter's salary. This brings us down to £700 as the clear reward received by the two partners (£350 each) as the mere result of the combination. But we have not done yet. The foreman was guaranteed his salary whether the business had been successful or not, and it must therefore be put down as outlay; not so with the managing partner's. This gives us £12,500 received as against £11,600 invested, or about $23\frac{1}{4}$ per cent. per annum. Deducting the managing partner's salary we have about 18 per cent. per annum, or 6 per cent. per single process of four months, as the result of the combination.

So far as trade is concerned we have now done; but the plutologist is not satisfied till he ascertains a few further particulars. What proportion, he asks, of this 18 per cent. appertains to the two combiners as the increment of value due to their own selves? The answer is simple. If £1,000 was spent on an engine, the proprietor of the engine is entitled at the end of the year to the profit due to it, and so with all other elements, the combiners included. But how do we know the value of the combiners? If they were likewise the owners of the other elements, it is true we cannot tell what their value was; but if they were not, it is clear some contract as to their value must have been previously entered into, and whatever their utility, their value is only and simply what they will fetch in the market.

No doubt if, after the process is complete, it is suspected that the increment of new value is mainly due to any particular element, the value of that element, whether combiner or anything else, will rise.

No doubt if any combiner possesses the power of inspiring his friends or the public with a belief in his permanent and certain solvency, that power is one amongst others of his valuable attributes. He can borrow at the current rate of interest (that is, at the average profit of the day), and then whatever profit results from his undertaking over and above that which is required to pay the interest on his borrowings must be regarded as the share of increased value due to himself.

In order to ascertain the profit on a given combination the plutologist puts down the value of the product, and then deducts from it the values of its ingredients — namely, the coals, the raw material, the oil, &c., the use or hire of the engines and other machinery, the mill and ground, &c., the horses and human workers of all sorts, including the combiners. The difference is the profit on the undertaking, the increment of new value due to the combination. Many of the labourers sell themselves to the combiner out and out for the time being—in other words, they let themselves out for hire at a fixed price. The engines, &c., are sometimes let out in precisely the same way, for a fixed time at a fixed price, but more frequently they are sold to the combiner as his permanent property. Foremen, managers, superintendents, and such like, form no exception. All such as receive fixed salaries thereby become for the time being the property (in a plutological sense) of the proprietor, who guarantees the salary. It is only in those very frequent cases in which the value of the combiner is not set down to outlay that any difficulty arises, and one is apt to forget that the mere act of calculating chances and scheming combinations is a labour, distinct from that of superintendence, but none the less a labour; and the fact that some foremen perform this difficult function does not entitle all foremen as such to the name of combiner.

The reward of risk is the reward of the combiner. He who would receive more than current interest for his property must judge for himself, and if he judges wisely he proves his value. The risk of a combination is a measure of the ability, the value of the combiner.

## CHAPTER IX.

### LAWS OF VALUE.

THE mere consideration of the different kinds of wealth from the point of view adopted in this treatise has compelled us to regard them as related to one another in certain very definite ways. We have spoken of the elements of a compound, and the simple statement involves the idea of a definite relation subsisting between the substances styled elements and the substances styled compound.

Again, the substances which enter together into the same compound stand to one another in a definite relation, precisely that in which hydrogen stands to oxygen in the compound called water. I am not aware that chemists are agreed upon the name most suitable to express this latter relation. The term components is frequently used either as synonymous with elements or as an adjective in conjunction with elements; but never, so far as I know, in the sense of co-element or partner in the combination. Oxygen is never styled the component of hydrogen in the composition of water. In the absence of any less ambiguous term I shall employ co-element to indicate this coadjutorship. Oxygen is the co-element of hydrogen in the composition of water; water is the compound of oxygen and hydrogen. Oxygen and hydrogen are the elements of water.

There can be no mistake in employing these terms,

K

and, at the risk of tautology, I shall henceforth use them to the exclusion of all synonyms; for although we may do good work with an inferior nomenclature by means of accurate definitions, still it is always better to employ a clear and symmetrical one at any sacrifice of style when treating of scientific subjects.

From the science of chemistry I have borrowed the terms compound, proximate element, and ultimate element to connote the homologous plutological relations, and in the absence of any precise technical term in chemistry I have adopted that of co-element to signify the relation in which one ingredient in any compound stands to all the other ingredients.

But there is yet another relation subsisting between substances of value which must not be overlooked, or the most disastrous confusions will result. This is the relation of substitutes, rivals, or competitors.

In a general analysis of clothes we should rightly split the compound up into machinery, labourers, textile fabrics, &c.; and we might at first sight possibly feel tempted to analyse textile fabrics into cotton, wool, flax, silk, &c. This would of course be to confound enumeration with analysis, just as if a chemist should give as the result of his analysis of earths in general, baryta, strontia, lime, magnesia, &c., instead of metal and oxygen. This is an error into which we cannot possibly fall if we invariably avoid general analyses until we have paved the way by the preparation of a number of special.

It is now time to enunciate the laws of value.

In works on political economy we are told that the

temporary or market value of a commodity is that at which the effectual demand for it equals the supply of it. This form, for which I believe we are indebted to Mill, is certainly more intelligible than its acknowledged predecessor, "The value of a thing is the ratio between supply and demand."

Yet even the improved formula conveys but a vague notion. What *is* the demand for a thing?

Once for all, argues Mill, let us dispense with the qualifying term "effectual." With any other than effectual demand political economy can have nothing to do. Even to the uninitiated in political economy an extensive demand for silk goods does not mean that crowds of poor people would gladly possess silk gowns if they could get them for nothing. It means simply that there are plenty of persons able and willing to purchase silk goods at their market value; and effectual demand can mean nothing more.

But this effectual demand, how is it measured? Is it the number of persons who buy the article? No, for it depends upon the amounts purchased. Fifty persons buying three pounds of tea each constitute a larger demand than a hundred persons buying one pound each.

It appears, then, that the demand for a commodity is the total amount of it *purchased*. And the supply is the total amount of it for sale. Hence the value of a thing is that at which the amount purchased equals the amount for sale. And yet there is more meaning in the law than that. For if the value were lower the amount purchased would equal the amount for sale. It could not be greater, and naturally it would not be less.

What is meant to be conveyed is in fact this—that the whole of the supply is sold, and yet nobody who desires to have some or more of the article *at the price* is left without. This would not be the case if the value were lowered.

It is difficult, if not impossible, to explain this conception more clearly than, and at the same time as concisely as, is done by saying that the value is that at which the demand equals the supply, but it is equally difficult to understand this statement without further explanation.

In the first place sellers and buyers are not two classes, but one class. Everything of value is sold. It is nonsense even to talk of part of the supply remaining unsold when the value is too high. To refuse a certain price for an article is to give that price for it. A proprietor who refuses to sell a horse for fifty guineas virtually gives fifty guineas for the horse in the hope of getting more for him another day, or else because he obtains more gratification from the horse than from fifty guineas. Proprietors who do not sell must be regarded as virtually buyers of their own goods. Hence the supply must always equal the demand. For it was seen that though the value be supposed too low, yet the demand (that is, of course, the effectual demand) cannot possibly exceed the supply. More of a thing cannot be bought than exists. And now it appears that though the value be supposed too high, yet the supply cannot possibly exceed the demand, because the whole of the supply must be virtually sold. So that when carefully scrutinised the proposition that the market value of a thing is that at which the demand for it equals the supply of it turns out to be meaningless and absurd.

I have already explained what is intended to be understood by this formula in plain English, and it may be shown to involve three distinct propositions which it will be as well to unravel and consider separately.

1. The value of a thing is the greatest amount of any other thing, or of things in general, which can be obtained in exchange for it.

2. The total supply of every valuable is necessarily sold.

3. Every unit of it is sold at the same value.

I use the word unit instead of portion or fraction because many commodities cannot be subdivided for purposes of sale into less than very considerable units, such as a piano, a horse, &c.

It will be observed that the first of these three propositions is simply the definition of value. The price at which a thing will be sold is assumed to be the highest price at which it can be sold. Nobody denies that some things are sold "for an old song," and some given away gratis. Such events conform to laws with which plutology has not to deal.

The second proposition is obvious on bearing in mind what has just been pointed out—that proprietors who do not sell are virtually buyers.

The third proposition is the fundamental one. It

is an abstract rather than a general law. Like the laws of motion enunciated by Newton, it represents an invariable tendency, but is never actually conformed to.

After the elimination of disturbing causes, which never are really absent, this law holds good. It is the result of competition, which plutology assumes to be ever in active operation, levelling values as gravitation levels the sea. Without accepting as a datum the fact of competition, we should of course be unable to form any idea of value, which is, as has been explained, the amount of any one thing for which any other thing has been ascertained by experience to be exchangeable. As was shown at the time, competition alone could bring about those admitted ratios. A flour-merchant may have given twice as much for one sack of flour as for another of the same quality, but he will be obliged to sell both at the same price to his customers. Facts tend to conform more and more nearly to this law as the machinery of trade becomes more lubricated; yet even now it is at the worst as true in the concrete as the first law of motion.

Now from these simple and very intelligible propositions our plain English interpretation of Mill's market value equation is easily deducible. For if all the units of a commodity are necessarily sold, and each of them at the highest value they will respectively fetch in the market, it is clear that nobody is left as it were out in the cold desiring to give a higher value for any of the commodity than it has been sold to others for.

In future, therefore, after this scrutiny we shall find it advisable to dispense with the term "demand" altogether. Indeed, the word has caused much confusion of thought, and it is a very good riddance. How often are we asked to consider the consequences of an increased demand for such a commodity! Now, bearing in mind what *demand* means, how can we conceive of an increased demand for anything? How can more of an article be effectually demanded—*i.e.*, not only desired, but bought—than actually exists? The only conceivable meaning to be attached to such an expression is an increased value due to a stimulated desire to possess the article in question, on account, say, of a change of fashion, or what not. How much better, then, to speak plainly and to talk of a rise of value instead of an increased demand! If it is wished to explain the cause of the raised value, why not do it in simple language instead of by implication? Surely it is easy enough to affirm that the enhanced value of coal at a certain date was due to its increased desirableness on account of the low temperature, and not to a rise in the values of any of its elements of production. Nothing could be clearer; and the erroneous and absurd notion of an extended area of consumption as a prime cause is at once rendered inconceivable. As a fact, an extended area of consumption, or, in plain English, a larger supply—a larger quantity of the commodity—is the last link in a chain of cause and effect, and not, as is sometimes supposed, the first. Stimulated desire causes raised value; raised value gives large increment of value on the combination. Large profits render it practicable for other combiners to combine additional elements (such as transport) in their compounds, and yet leave average profits; thus results an augmented supply, and, what is the same thing, an extended consumption.

Perhaps the above and succeeding remarks will be understood best by those who have read little or nothing of political economy. In order to form clear ideas of value we must dismiss from our minds all the notions and pseud-concepts so familiar to our ears, if not to our understanding. We must unlearn all we have learnt about demand and supply, about buyers and sellers, about temporary and permanent values, and we must simply remember that there is a certain amount of every valuable commodity in existence, neither more nor less; nor can it be increased by a single atom, though the whole population suddenly, as if by inspiration, began craving and yearning for it. What the eventual results of such a craving might or might not be we are not just now concerned with; we only want to perceive how the value of existing things (what Mill calls their temporary value) is determined. To do this perhaps the best plan is to eliminate the idea of proprietorship altogether. Suppose everything of value to be piled up in heaps at a certain spot, and belonging to no one. Suppose the population to resort to that spot under the following agreements:—That the commodities shall be sold separately by auction in small portions; that every portion of the same commodity shall be sold at the same price; and that that price shall be the highest bid.

Money must be supposed to be unequally distributed amongst the purchasers gathered together. Counters would answer the purpose as well or better —namely, that of representing the different purchasing powers of different persons—a fact already admitted as a plutological datum. I will, however, express the counters in money terms for the sake of simplicity.

Picture this population of 250 persons, say, gathered together at a monster auction at which every desirable commodity under the sun is offered for sale, and unattainable elsewhere. There stand the purchasers of every gradation of wealth, from those at the bottom with, say, one penny each, to those at the top with a million pounds sterling. The first article put up is bread, divided into portions or loaves equal to the daily requirements of the average individual. First, it is observed that, whereas the population or purchasers number 250, the loaves, on the other hand, number only 230. Now the bidding commences. Every one desires one loaf. No one desires more than one. A penny! No, that won't do. Fifty persons must in that case be left breadless, though willing and able to pay. Twopence! No, not enough yet. Threepence! fourpence! Now it happens that out of the 250 persons there are 20 with only one penny each and 10 with only twopence; the remainder having fourpence or more each. It is clear the penny and twopenny folks are already outbidden, but inasmuch as half a loaf is better than no bread, they club together—the penny folks in fours, and the twopenny folks in twos—and go on bidding fourpence a loaf. The hammer falls. Fourpence is the value of the loaf. The penny folks take 5 loaves among 20 of them, a quarter of a loaf each. The twopenny folks take other 5 amongst 10 of them, and the remaining 220 persons take one loaf each. Thus the 230 loaves are sold and the 250 persons accommodated according to their means.

The next article put up is the stock of hats. All those persons who came with only fourpence or less in their pockets are of course already knocked out of the market. They have spent their all. 205 persons are left to bid for the hats which all desire to possess. Twopence! sixpence! a shilling! No, there are only 150 hats. Now there are two points of difference between this case and that of the bread. First, when once the bid has risen beyond a man's individual means, he ceases to demand; he does not club with another and rest content with half or a quarter of a hat. Second, when the bid has exceeded a certain price, certain persons, who would otherwise desire the hat at a moderate consideration, though able to bid higher, prefer to keep their money for other commodities, whereas the need for bread was paramount.

And now half-a-dozen carriages come on for sale. Ten, twenty, thirty pounds are offered. Only ten persons continue to bid. Fifty, sixty, sixty-five. Only seven bidders remain. Seventy, eighty, eighty-two, eighty-three.  Another party ceases to bid, and the six carriages are knocked down to the six remaining competitors at £84 pounds apiece.

Finally, there is a large diamond to be sold. Naturally enough the bidding goes on till there is but one left who will give more than £340; he offers £341, and carries off the gem.

And so with all the other commodities.

The value of each article is that at which the last of the outbidden *stuck*.

So much for the present value, or what is called the temporary or market value of commodities. Now this value is the only one of which we do or can know anything.  The value of a thing *is* its market value, nor has it any other.  We are told, however, that of far more importance than this temporary value is the *permanent* value—the *natural* value of a thing.

The origin of this belief in a permanent value first requires accounting for.  No one supposes that values are constant; on the contrary, they are ever fluctuating, and their oscillations, as might be predicted, are rhythmical.  The surface of the sea affords a parallel illustration.  First we have the ripples playing over the waves.  The particles of water are now higher now lower than the surface of the wave, but on the average the elevations and depressions cancel each other.  But we do not suppose that the surface of the wave is at a constant level. The ripple that was just now on the crest is now in the trough of the wave.  The cork that rises and falls as the wave passes along rises the same distance above as it falls below the average surface of the water at that particular hour. But is the broader surface even always at the same level? By no means. Twice a day we have high tide and twice a day low tide; nor even when these oscillations are averaged do we obtain a constant level. There are the spring tides and the neap tides, and not only these but the highest and lowest spring tides, and so forth. Nor must we lose sight of the gradual elevations and depressions of the land which, in alternate millions of ages, coop up the water in deeper and narrower basins and spread it over wider and shallower ones. And if this unrest, this perpetual oscillation about a centre which itself oscillates about another centre, which again oscillates about a third, and so forth—if, I say, this unrest is so noticeable in a case like the surface of the ocean where so few causes are at work—wind, moon, and sun—what shall we think of those who talk of a permanent value about which market values oscillate continually?

No doubt market values do oscillate very irregularly about a centre, which itself oscillates even more irregularly about some other; but such is the number and force of disturbing causes at work that we cannot safely attempt to find even the second or wave-level, much less any of those alternating through longer periods. And even if we did succeed in finding approximately such second level by a system of averages, we should certainly not be justified in styling it the permanent value.

This, however, accounts sufficiently for the origin of the notion. We may now pass on to the consideration of the method by which it has been attempted to ascertain this so-called permanent or natural value. (From Aristotle downwards this term "natural" has ever been employed to designate pseud-concepts.) First of all, commodities, we are told, fall into three classes, according to their difficulty of attainment. First, those which are not indefinitely multipliable. Second, those which are indefinitely multipliable, but not at a proportionate outlay. Third, those which are indefinitely multipliable at a proportionate outlay. Concerning the natural value of the first class we are left in the dark or driven to conjecture that it coincides with their market value; but of the second and third classes we are told that their permanent value is determined by the cost of production, with a qualification in the case of the second class.

I have said that every commodity of value is limited in amount, from the air we breathe to the jewels we wear, but in very different degrees; and that the value of the commodity depends, other things equal, upon the absolute amount of it procurable. Put in a negative form, to employ the terms in vogue amongst economists, the value of anything depends on the difficulty of its attainment.

According to Mill, as I have said, there are three kinds of difficulty of attainment; but, in order to avoid misrepresentation, I will quote his explanation of them *in extenso*.

"The ifficulty of attainment which determines value is not always the same kind of difficulty. It sometimes consists in an absolute limitation of the supply. There are things of which it is physically impossible to increase the quantity beyond certain narrow limits. Such are those wines which can be grown only in peculiar circumstances of soil, climate, and exposure. Such also are ancient sculptures, pictures by old masters, rare books or coins, or other articles of antiquarian curiosity. Among such may also be reckoned houses and building-ground in a town of definite extent (such as Venice or any fortified town where fortifications are necessary to security); the most desirable sites in any town whatever; houses and parks peculiarly favoured by natural beauty in places where that advantage is uncommon. Potentially all land whatever is a commodity of this class, and might be practically so in countries fully occupied and cultivated.

"But there is another category (embracing the majority of all things that are bought and sold) in which the obstacle to attainment consists only in the labour and expense requisite to produce the commodity. Without a certain labour and expense it cannot be had; but when any one is willing to incur these there needs be no limit to the multiplication of the product. If there were labourers enough and machinery enough, cottons, woollens, or linens might be produced by thousands of yards for every single yard now manufactured. There would be a point, no doubt, where further increase would be stopped by the incapacity of the earth to afford more of the material. But there is no need for any purpose of political economy to contemplate a time when this ideal limit could become a practical one.

"There is a third case intermediate between the two preceding, and rather more complex, which I shall at present merely indicate, but the importance of which in political economy is extremely great. There are commodities which can be multiplied to an indefinite extent by labour and expenditure, but not by a fixed amount of labour and expenditure. Only a limited quantity can be produced at a given cost; if more is wanted it must be produced at a greater cost. To this class, as has been often repeated, agricultural produce belongs, and generally all the rude produce of the earth; and this peculiarity is a source of very important consequences, one of which is the necessity of a limit to population, and another the payment of rent."

With respect to the law of value for the commodities in the first class, which, strange to say, he designates as exceptions, Mill's explanation is clear enough. The value of the article is the figure at which the demand for it equals the supply of it. He wisely discards the expression "ratio" between demand and supply. We speak rightly, says he, not of a *ratio*, but of an *equation*.

Before proceeding to treat of the cause of the value of those commodities which he describes as susceptible of indefinite multiplication without increase of cost, and of the law relating thereto, which is none other than the law that value is determined by cost of production, Mill admits that even such commodities may all of them fall temporarily into the first class. Thus all monopolised articles, and even articles which during a certain interval cannot be increased, such as all the corn in the world till next harvest. "In the case of *most* commodities it requires a certain time to increase their quantity; and if the demand increases, then until a corresponding supply can be brought forward—that is, until the supply can accommodate itself to the demand—the value will so rise as to accommodate the demand to the supply." But this is not all. Not only does this class of so-called exceptions already contain all things the like of which cannot possibly be reproduced at all; all monopolised articles; and all articles whatever during certain periods (which periods, by the way, are almost always current), but further, "there are commodities of which, though capable of being increased or diminished to a great and even an unlimited extent, the value never depends upon anything but demand and supply. This is the case in particular with the commodity labour." Surely our exceptions bid fair to devour the rule; but as if the above categories were not enough, we are told that "there are many cases besides in which we shall find it necessary to call in this principle to solve difficult questions of exchange value. This will be particularly exemplified when we treat of international values."

Let us now follow Mill as he proceeds to explain the law of value for those things which can be increased at pleasure. In their case, says he, "it is strictly correct to say that their value does not depend (except accidentally and during the time necessary for production to adjust itself) upon demand and supply; on the contrary, *demand and supply depend upon it.*" According to him and the received doctrine, cost of production determines value, and value determines supply and demand. The reader may be supposed to be familiar with the chain of reasoning upon which this conclusion hangs, and if he is not he may consult Mill's *Principles of Political Economy*, Book III., c. iii., where he will find it admirably set forth. And indeed there is a great deal of truth in the arguments there put forward, which renders the conclusion all the more dangerous.

But first of all suppose the demand for any one of the commodities susceptible of multiplication to cease entirely. What is the result? "Oh, that is impossible, for inasmuch as the demand depends upon the value—*i.e.* on the cost of production—it cannot be supposed to cease." Nevertheless, *as matter of fact* the demand for commodities of this sort has been known to cease, and the consequence of its cessation was, as a fact, a fall in the value almost to zero without any perceptible change in the cost of production. Instances of a great diminution in the demand for such commodities altogether unoccasioned by an alteration in cost of production are to be witnessed daily. Sealskin jackets have this very year gone down considerably, owing to change of fashion, although the cost of their production is, if anything, slightly higher than heretofore.

Again, an increased desire for a commodity brings about a rise in the value of such commodities, as all admit, and this is usually followed by an increased production, which, as I do not deny, frequently lowers the value again to its original amount. And this is the point to which I wish to draw particular attention. Frequently the value is brought back to its original level, I say; frequently it falls *almost* but not quite to that level; frequently it falls considerably below that level. Perhaps the last consequence is the most frequent.

And each of these consequences, be it noted, is lasting. Hence the cost of production is affected by an increased desire for an indefinitely-augmentable commodity. And it is affected in opposite ways. Sometimes it is increased, sometimes diminished. How is this? The explanation is not difficult. Two forces are at work, and according as one of them is greater, equal, or less than the other, the cost is higher, equal, or lower than before the increased desire, or, in other words, the increased utility of the article.

The direct tendency of a stimulated desire for *any commodity whatever* is to raise its value. But this tendency may be, and usually is, mitigated or neutralised, or altogether outweighed, by an indirect consequence of the same antecedent. That indirect consequence is the well-known *economy* rendered possible by manufacture on a large scale. The larger the demand is, the larger the scale on which an indefinitely-augmentable commodity can be manufactured; and the larger this scale is, the greater the opportunity afforded for the organisation and differentiation of the work. Co-operation, division of labour, invention, and all the other results of manufacture on a large scale, come in, and, as I have stated, not only mitigate but neutralise, and even still more frequently quite overcome, the tendency of the increased desire to raise the value of the commodity in question.

The neutralisation wholly or partly of these two opposing tendencies in the case of most manufactured articles has very naturally given rise to the belief that the demand for such articles does not determine their value; and the very formidable exceptions which agricultural products presented to the erroneous law based on such belief necessitated the creation of a third class—a third kind of difficulty of attainment. To my mind the very existence and description of this third class ought to have set political economists a-thinking whether, after all, there might not be something wrong about this law of cost determining what they style natural value.

This third class is said to comprehend those articles which, although susceptible of indefinite multiplication, can only be increased at a greater proportional cost. Corn and agricultural produce generally are included under this head, and certainly it is the case with these articles that an increased supply of one-tenth can only be obtained by an increased cost of considerably more than one-tenth. In the case of corn the effect of an increased requirement in raising the value is more than sufficient to counteract the opposite tendency due to division of labour, &c., and it is, therefore, so marked as to require explanation; but, as I have said, the same law holds good of all commodities whatsoever. A stimulated desire for cotton goods really raises the value of such goods a little; for raw cotton is required in greater abundance, and, as a consequence, cotton-growing land, which rises to meet the demand. Such, however, is the advantage of manufacturing cotton goods on a large scale, rendering possible a separation of the several processes and their consequent simplification and adaptation to mechanical treatment, that the actual and visible result is an eventually lowered value. Between cotton goods and wheaten loaves, however, there are articles of all degrees in this respect. That is to say, on a stimulated desire for them, cotton goods eventually go down considerably, corn goes up considerably, while other things rise a little and sink a little, and others, again, keep their level. Thus the second and third classes merge into one another; and no one would like to assert, for example, whether dried figs and currants fall into one or the other. And if thus there is no hard and fast line to be drawn between the second and third kinds of difficulty of attainment, so also it is impossible to draw a line between these and the first class.

After all, at best this classification of commodities is a strange one. 'Surely economists do not mean to persuade us that the first class never vary in value—

that their market value is their permanent value. If they do not mean this, all they can mean is that cost of production does not determine the value of such commodities, and there is no knowing what does. All three classes appear to have their temporary values determined in the same way.

And again, when we put a few simple questions as to the meaning of cost of production, the answers we receive are at best vague and confusing. Here is a quantity of spun cotton which cost twenty guineas the making. Is that the value of it? No; you can get an equal quantity of similar stuff for fifteen shillings, simply because since it was made a machine has been invented for manufacturing it at this price. Oh, it is not the cost of producing the article which determines its value, but the cost of producing its like at the present time. This is qualification the first.

Here is a racehorse, favourite for the coming St. Leger, or here is a vocalist of rare talent. What is the estimated cost of producing another like them? Or, in the case of an ordinary full-grown carthorse, value fifty pounds, will it cost fifty pounds to produce another like him or of the same value? No; the breeder has to be recouped on the animals he rears for the losses he sustains on those that fail, die, or fall lame. But this is no element in the cost of the successful horse. Ah, but you must calculate, not the cost of the article, but the average expense incurred in producing a number like it. This is qualification the second. If you proceed to adduce the case of a coal-pit, a newly-found gold-nugget, or a patented invention, and ask whether the cost of sinking the shaft, of travelling to the diggings, of taking out the patent, actually represent the respective values of these treasures, you are reminded that every rule has its exceptions, and that these instances have already been classed together as exceptions to the rule in question. They are instances of the first class of commodities, though how or in what sense it can be said that a patented invention is a commodity not susceptible of indefinite multiplication passes all comprehension. But it is quite enough to be told that our calculations are to be based, not on the known cost of the existing article, but on the unknown cost of an article yet to be created, to satisfy us that, if such is the only method of discovering the natural or permanent value, we may as well rest content without attempting to learn it, especially when it is remembered that the very fact of creating the article in question will alone effect a change in the factors of the calculation.

If, then, we cannot discover the secondary, much less the permanent, value of a commodity by reason of the number and importance of disturbing and unforeseeable circumstances, let us content ourselves with the enunciation of some simple laws by means of which we may be enabled to calculate and predict the variations in the value of a given commodity under given conditions. Such a course is surely more practical, and at the same time more scientific, than the more ambitious one just described and condemned.

But before proceeding to do this let me recapitulate in a few words what I have endeavoured to expound in the last few pages. In the first place I have discarded the term *demand*, in its technical signification, as useless and misleading, and whenever I have since employed it, it has been entirely synonymous with *desire*. An extended or increased demand for a commodity means, in the sense in which I use it, simply a stimulated desire for it, owing to its increased utility. Utility, remember, embraces what some might call fancied or supposed utility, for if anything is supposed by the consumer to afford pleasure it needs must do so. How, it may be asked, can sable fur please more than sealskin one winter and less another? It must be fancy. Not at all; the lady who dresses in the fashion is more admired and envied, as a fact, than the lady who wears the fashions of a year ago. Hence the former actually does derive more gratification from a fashionable fur than from any other equally warm one. Desire for a thing means, then, that the thing desired is useful— that is, gratificable — and, as has been stated in a previous chapter, other things equal, the more useful a thing is (in the plutological sense) the more valuable it is. Hence when I speak of an extended demand or stimulated desire for any commodity, I mean simply that, for some reason or other, a higher value is attached to it than aforetime.

It is true, therefore, for all commodities whatsoever, that a stimulated desire for them *tends* to raise their value permanently—that is to say, for as long as they continue to be held in the same heightened estimation. Contrariwise, a contracted demand for them tends to lower their value.

But this tendency is sometimes mitigated, sometimes neutralised, and sometimes overcome by an indirect consequence of extended demand—viz., economy of production. Further, the resultant of the opposing forces differs in direction and intensity with different commodities, and it is utterly useless and misleading for purposes of classification. In other words, there are not three kinds of difficulty of attainment, but an infinite number of degrees of difficulty, from that of obtaining commodities like broadcloth, for which a greatly-extended demand has resulted in an immense reduction in value, to antique chinas, a slight extension in the demand for certain sorts of which has resulted of late in a tenfold rise in value.

We will now proceed to consider the relations subsisting between the varying values of different articles. A complete dearth of special analyses precludes us from even attempting to lay down any laws governing the mutual relations of particular commodities; but a few general laws may be enunciated which can easily be shown to hold good in the abstract—that is to say, so far as regards the tendency of the variations, though subject to important qualifications due to disturbing causes, when applied to the concrete.

*First Law.* A rise in the value of a compound is followed by a rise in the values of its several elements, but not necessarily at the same rate. A fall in the compound is also followed by a fall in the latter.

*Second Law.* A rise in the value of an element

is followed by a rise in the value of its compounds, and a fall by a fall, but not necessarily at the same rate.

*Third Law.* Other things equal, a rise in the value of a co-element is followed by a fall in the values of its co-elements, and a fall by a rise, but not necessarily at the same rate.

*Fourth Law.* Other things equal, a rise in the value of any commodity is followed by a rise in the value of its substitutes, and a fall by a fall, but not necessarily at the same rate.

Expressed more briefly, compounds and elements vary directly as each other, but at different rates.

Co-elements vary inversely as one another, but at different rates. Substitutes vary directly as each other.

The condition "other things equal" is obviously necessary, for if the rise in value of a compound should be followed by an equal and simultaneous rise in the values of all its elements, it is clear that these co-elements would not be varying inversely as one another. Similarly with the other relations.

The above laws require illustration.

Here is black ink, consisting of Aleppo galls, sulphate of iron, gum-arabic, and water. The water having no value may be neglected, and so also may the small element of labourers contained in the compound. Now if the spread of education should impart a higher value to the ink, the values of the three elements enumerated will rise also, but not proportionately. Of the sulphate of iron the rise in value will be imperceptible; of the gum-arabic, slight; and of the galls very considerable, greater even than that of the ink itself. All three will, nevertheless, tend to rise in value, but, in the words of the law, not necessarily at the same rate. In this case the raised values of the elements are due to the raised value of the compound.

But suppose an independent rise to take place in the value of Aleppo galls, due to one of the only two causes possible — either a scarcity of them or increased utility, such as would result from a discovery rendering them available for dyeing purposes. What is the effect of such an independent rise on the values of the ink and of the sulphate of iron and gum-arabic? Firstly, the creation of a new supply of ink is decreased, because combiners perceive that the value of the ink, after paying for the elements, including the galls at the new value, will leave but a small increment of new value or profit, or maybe none at all. Consequently they will some of them cease to perform the combination, and the supply will diminish. Certain persons who formerly used it can no longer be provided with it, or at least, not with the same quantity, and those who will have it must outbid the others. Hence the value of the ink is raised and its supply diminished.

But if less ink is created, clearly less sulphate of iron and gum-arabic are required; and since all the supply must be sold and a smaller equivalent is forthcoming, it is obvious that their values will be lowered. These results coincide with the second and third laws as above enunciated.

The fourth law requires a fuller explanation. Woollen goods frequently contain large quantities of cotton, and the mixtures have special names, and are, indeed, distinct commodities. Now a cold winter, causing a stimulated desire and consequent raised value of wool, would, according to law three, tend to lower that of its co-element cotton in such mixed fabrics. As a fact, however, this is not the case. The fourth law comes into play. Cotton is to a great extent a substitute for wool, and it averages less than half the price as imported raw; hence those poorer persons who cannot afford the higher price for the wool make shift with cotton. This stimulated desire for cotton raises its value. This is an example of conflicting tendencies. Two laws are at work. In obedience to both the tendency is there, but the one tendency is stronger than the other. It is the case of an iron filing rising to the magnet in opposition to the force of gravity. It obeys both laws. It would strike the magnet with greater force if held below the filing than if held above it.

Let us not, then, overlook the fact that the same commodities may be and are at the same time acting in different capacities—standing in double relations to one another—that of co-elements and that of substitutes.

A very remarkable example of this kind of double relation has been presented to us during the present century, and it is only lately that the majority of manual labourers have discovered the truth. I refer to the relation subsisting in most branches of manufacture between hand-workers and machinery. There is no disputing the obvious fact that rivalry exists between the two; they can be used and are used as substitutes the one for the other. It requires no keen insight to perceive this, and upon the introduction of machinery towards the close of the last and all through the first half of the present century into the factories of every species of ware, the fiercest and most strenuous opposition was made to it. No arguments were required to demonstrate to the hand-weaver that if the power-loom could do the same amount of work per day as he could, and at a smaller cost than he was in the habit of receiving as wage, he must either be beaten out of the field or submit to a reduction of his pay. Who shall blame him for resisting his supposed enemy with all his force, by foul means as well as by fair? To him it was a matter of life and death. Infuriated mobs gathered together, machinery was smashed, inventors threatened and persecuted, and not a little blood was shed. The inventor of the wool-combing machine has related how, as late as the year 1848, he was compelled in self-defence to walk about with a loaded revolver in his hand; and even twenty years later, at a monster meeting of colliers in the West Riding of Yorkshire, a solemn litany was chanted invoking the Lord's help against the new enemy. "From the devil and all his works, from —— and the iron man, good Lord deliver us." This iron man was the name given to the first practical machine for cutting coal, and I have frequently found it "nobbled" in various ingenious ways by the colliers, when inspecting the working of some new improvement on behalf of the inventor. Sometimes sand was jammed into the pipe conveying the compressed air to the machine, sometimes fine nails were wedged fast in between the piston-rod and cylinder-end, and even bribery was resorted to, and the men at the air-pump above were induced to lower the pressure required for the machine. In most branches of industry, however, this kind of warfare is out of fashion, and it is for us to explain this change of attitude. Indeed, the cry of protection for inventions and cheap patents has, of late, become a working-man's cry, and those who would abolish patent right are regarded with extreme jealousy by the artisan.

The explanation is not far to seek. A few statistics are quite sufficient for the purpose. Any one who will take the trouble to ascertain how many operatives were employed in the British woollen trade before the introduction of machinery, or even as late as in 1845, and compare that number with the 170,000 employed in the year 1861 and the 300,000 employed at the present day, will hardly continue to fear for the working classes (as they are called) lest they should be "cut out" by machinery. Let him further compare the present wages of operatives with what they received in the glorious days of hand-labour, and further let him note particularly the swelled figures which invariably follow the invention of some new and revolutionising process. Let him run through the statistics of the stocking trade, the iron trade, the glass trade, and in every instance he will discover that cheap and effective machinery tends, not to throw labourers out of work (at least never for very long), but eventually and speedily to increase the demand for them to a surprising extent, so as to bring about a startling rise both in their numbers and their value.

It appears, then, that it is not as substitutes that we must primarily regard machinery and labourers, but as co-elements, each requiring the assistance of the other in the creation of the compound.

Now, according to the third law of value, the values of co-elements vary, other things equal, inversely. Hence a fall in the value of machinery due to new invention, by causing an extended demand for its compounds, indirectly raises the value of labourers. Time alone was requisite to teach the workman this fact. At first, of course, the tendency of the fourth law following more quickly upon the employment of machinery than the more permanent and stronger tendency of the third law, was held more prominently before him, and took firmer hold of his imagination. The reconciliation of these two great elements may be said to date roughly from the middle of the present century.

Upon the laws of value I will say no more. Indeed, we can never pretend to proceed far when we have no better instrument of discovery than deduction in dealing with concrete facts so heterogeneous as those of wealth.

The general laws of value and those of decreasing generality will be found by induction when sufficient ground has been cleared by analysis to afford foothold. We must ascend from the particular to the general, and from the general to the more general; but, as was admitted in the chapter on method, we can do no harm by deducing certain obvious laws from what we do know and by the aid of common sense. At the same time, as the example of wool and cotton just cited shows, we must always be very careful not to rely too trustfully on the application to the concrete of abstract laws which inform us concerning tendencies, in the absence of general laws which inform us concerning facts. May a future not remote reveal some of these laws to us!

## CHAPTER X.
### CLASSIFICATION.

PARI PASSU with the advance of plutological analysis and the progressive discovery of general laws of value a consistent classification of the kinds of wealth may be expected to organise itself. At present any attempt on my part to present even the nucleus of one would be premature, based, as it needs must be, chiefly on guess-work. Guesses are not always wrong, but a too free use of them is at best dangerous. One would not, for example, be far wrong probably in surmising that a horse and a diamond would fall under categories far apart. An actress and a ton of coals would also keep at a distance from each other. Take the following list of species and try to classify them roughly:—Wool, horses, wheat, tinkers, pineapples, statues, barristers, looms, violins, actresses, diamonds, cattle, coals, lapdogs, mutton, files, streets, ships, soil, old chinas, bank-notes, lace, note-paper. If three of us attempt it separately no two would in all probability be even approximately alike.

One would place the human beings, tinkers, barristers, and actresses, in one class; the horses, cattle, and dogs in a second; the wheat and pineapples in a third; the wool and mutton, possibly, with the animals, or in a separate class; and the remaining inorganic articles in two classes according as they might be called raw or manufactured articles; the latter embracing the statues, looms, violins, files, ships, chinas, with misgivings as to the ships (being of wood), serious misgivings as to whether lace and paper should figure as vegetables, and utter discomfiture as to the proper place of paper bank-notes. The streets, too, would sorely puzzle this biologically-biassed *savant*.

A second classifier versed in the doctrines of political economy would ask himself whether the respective articles are intended for productive or unproductive consumption. The answer would split up the group into two classes possibly enough dubbed capital and not-capital. The former would embrace the wool, wheat, tinkers, looms, cattle, coals, mutton, files, streets, ships, soil. The latter, pineapples, statues, violins, actresses, diamonds, lapdogs, old chinas, lace. Labelled doubtful would be the horses (depending on their kind, race or cart horses), the barristers, the note-paper, and, lastly, the bank-notes.

A third would ask whether the respective articles in question are permanent or evanescent, and he would refuse to classify the human beings at all, as being, not wealth, but that for which wealth exists. He would then divide the residue somehow thus: wool, wheat, pineapples, coals, mutton, note-paper, in one class; statues, looms, violins, diamonds, files, streets, ships, soil, old chinas, in a second class; horses, cattle, lace, and bank-notes in a third class as doubtful.

Now we might construct a table on the eclectic

M

principle in which all three parties should be represented; and possibly such a table might correspond in many particulars with the ultimate classification resulting from plutological research.

At the same time it is difficult to see what advantage is to accrue from the distinction between animals, vegetables, and minerals. Human beings, no doubt, may possibly constitute a class to themselves, inasmuch as they are proprietors as well as wealth, but even this reason is not convincing. We may easily ascertain the effect of given conditions upon any particular individual of a species, without elevating such individual to the dignity of a separate species. And although it is undeniable that anything which has a tendency to raise or lower the value of any considerable class of human beings is of great importance; still, unless it is found that such variations obey different laws from those to which changes in the values of horses and engines conform, there seems to be no reason for detaching them from their natural plutological kindred.

Again, those who would distinguish between vegetable and animal forms of wealth, or between mineral and vegetable, saddle themselves with gratuitous burdens. Shall coal rank with vegetables or minerals? Draw a line between soil, manure, milk, eggs, caviare. Classify pearls, coral beads, and sponges. Flannel and linen, too, seem to have far too much in common to warrant their being set so far apart as the division between vegetable and animal products would require. Not to multiply instances, I think I have made it pretty clear that nothing can damage plutology more than premature attempts at classification.

It is one thing to classify and another thing to define. We cannot have classification without diagnosis, but it does not follow that we cannot have rigorous diagnosis without classification. On the importance of precise definition I would lay great stress, calling attention at the same time to a certain false view of the subject of definitions in general which seems to have taken hold of the scientific mind at the present time. It is assumed by some that simply because we have admitted the theory of continuous development we are thereby precluded from drawing an absolute distinction—a hard and fast line between any two groups. They merge imperceptibly, we are told, one into another.

In the chapter on definitions in the late Professor Cairnes's *Logical Method of Political Economy* this notion seems to underlie his arguments in favour of the current nomenclature of political economy. His remarks were called forth, I have reason to believe, by a wish to vindicate that branch of study against the attack made upon it in the Essay on Capital which is inserted after this chapter. This essay was then, and has since remained, in the manuscript, never having been published. It contains the germ of the present work, and, as will be seen, I have thought it better not to make any alterations in it on bringing it before the public. I am aware that in many respects it is out of harmony with the theory and nomenclature of the other portions of this treatise, but it will serve the better to mark the transitional state of the science of wealth in passing from political economy to plutology. It bears the same relation to the present short treatise which it is to be hoped the latter will bear to some future and more complete work on the subject. But to return to Professor Cairnes's remarks on definitions:—

"In connection," he writes, "with the subject of classification a further remark must be made. In controversies about definitions nothing is more common than to meet objections founded on the assumption that the attribute on which a definition turns ought to be one which does not admit of degrees. This being assumed, the objector goes on to show that the facts or objects placed within the boundary-line of some definition to which exception is taken cannot in their extreme instances be clearly discriminated from those which lie without. Some equivocal example is thus taken, and the framer of the definition is challenged to say in which category it is to be placed. Now it seems to me that an objection of this kind ignores the inevitable conditions under which a scientific nomenclature is constructed, alike in political economy and in all the positive sciences. In such sciences nomenclature, and therefore definition, is based upon classification, and to admit of degrees is the character of all natural facts. As has been said, there are no hard lines in nature. Between the animal and vegetable kingdoms, for example, where is the line to be drawn? Vegetables only, it is true, decompose carbonic acid, but then all vegetables (*e.g.*, the fungi which obtain their carbon by feeding on other vegetables and some parasitic plants) do not do so. Some vegetables have motor actions like animals; and again, the lowest classes of animals have no muscles or nerves. 'If, then,' says Mr. Murphy, 'vegetables have motor actions like animals, and if there are whole tribes of vegetables which, like animals, do not decompose carbonic acid, and if the lowest class of animals have no muscles or nerves, what is the distinction between the kingdoms? I reply that I do not believe there is any absolute or certain distinction whatever!' External objects and events shade off into each other by imperceptible differences; and consequently definitions whose aim it is to classify such objects and events must of necessity be founded on circumstances partaking of this character."

I quote this paragraph in full, because it seems to me a most singular example of begging the question. Appealing, not to chemistry, but to natural history, we are told first that no hard and fast line can be drawn between animals and vegetables. Mr. Murphy is then dragged in to be held up to ridicule, because, forsooth, no distinction being definable, he refuses to acknowledge any distinction as subsisting in fact. Professor Huxley has recently made the same admission. But because there is no absolute distinction between the animal and vegetable kingdom, does that prove that there are no absolute distinctions anywhere? Does oxygen shade off into hydrogen, or water into oil? Or, to take whole classes, is there any imperceptible merging of the sulphides into the chlorates? But even in cases where there is a shading off, provided the intermediate links are missing or extinct, the most complete and exhaustive diagnosis can be made. Is there, then, an imperceptible shading off between men and rats? Produce all the intermediate types between the men, the rats, and their common ancestor, and it is admitted the line could not be drawn; but then the intermediate types are not to be found, and we have, consequently, no difficulty whatever in defining both rats and men. Have we any difficulty in pronouncing whether the most extreme and out-of-the-way creature discoverable is or is not a mammal or a bird? Even the bat of the fable no longer puzzles us. Again, can we not define red light so as to distinguish it from blue light, even though you take never so extreme an instance of each? Of the most orange shade of red and the greenest shade of blue we may always safely affirm that the vibrations are less numerous per second in the case of the former and more numerous in the case of the latter than those of pure yellow light. There is no overlapping in a case of this sort. So, likewise, of plutological facts. The value of one thing is due entirely to its power of entering into known compounds productively, and the value of another thing is due to its power of affording immediate gratification. Or again, to the utility of one thing its consumption is absolutely essential, of another thing merely accidental. There is no shading off here. Will any one produce an example of a commodity which stands as it were on neutral ground between these two? Is it suggested that pieces of coal and of iron ore are frequently placed in mineralogical collections and serve to instruct and gratify without being essentially consumed, whereas the consumption of these articles is essential to their general uses? True, but to which of these uses is their value due? Plutology treats of commodities in so far as they are valuable. And from this point of view there is no difficulty in pronouncing into which of the two categories any valuable falls, no more than there is in dividing the chemical elements into three distinct classes, according as they are liquid, solid, or gaseous at 50° Fahr. Surely there is something strange in the selection of biology from which to borrow the analogy. In almost all other instances Professor Cairnes was in the habit of pointing to chemistry, and, as it seems to me, rightly, for to no other science does plutology bear so marked a resemblance, both as to nature and method. Now, are the definitions in chemistry, let me again ask, " mere fictions founded on fact?" Do no such clearly-cut differences as those between nitrogen, bromine, and gold really exist in the actual universe? If external objects do actually shade off into each other by imperceptible degrees, where are the intermediate links between carbon and silver? Further illustration is needless to show that there is no such gradual merging to be found in the chemical world; and the admitted fact that it is to be found in the animal and vegetable worlds is attributable to the equally-admitted fact of evolution from a common stock. This genealogical relation, though of course subsisting between all kinds of wealth as between all animals and vegetables, is not in plutology, as it is in zoology and botany, the appropriate relation on which to base a classification. This is obvious when we bear in mind that the union of the most opposite and distinct kinds of wealth is frequently fertile, whereas in the animal and vegetable kingdoms this is by no means the case. If it were—if the most distinct genera and even orders and sub-kingdoms of animals were fertile *inter se*, clearly the genealogical relation would be not only inappropriate but as impracticable for a basis of classification in zoology as it is in mineralogy and plutology.

Hence in these two sciences we are compelled to fall back upon altogether different features as the salient ones according to which kinds are classed together or apart. In mineralogy it is difficult to pronounce on the most suitable; a chemical classification seems at present to prevail over a geological one, though the choice is, I think, open to grave objections. In plutology the best system is that based upon the laws to which the variations in value of different kinds of wealth conform. Consequently the study of these laws must precede a sound classification.

If I have spoken lightly either by name or by implication in the following essay of any who are no longer able to reply, it must be remembered that it was written a year and a-half ago, before the scientific and political world sustained losses not to be repaired in the death, first of Professor Cairnes, and shortly afterwards of Mr. G. Powlett Scrope. Both stood in the very first rank of political economists, together with Professor Fawcett, Professor Hearn, M. Chevalier, and M. Courcelle Seneuil; and to Professor Cairnes we are indebted for the admirable vindication of political economy as a true science, at a time when it bade fair to merge altogether into the chaos of empirical politics. If I have spoken in a slighting or disparaging manner of the writings or doctrines of any of the above authorities, I must plead the allowance usually made for articles intended for publication in periodicals, and for political and polemical discussions in general. The essay, as I have said, appears just as it was originally written, even the conventional "we" remaining unaltered.

# CAPITAL.

WHAT is capital? Surely many will complain that the conception is clearly defined already, or that the whole science of political economy must be rotten from the very foundation.

"If the nature of capital be thoroughly understood," writes Mr. John Macdonnel (*Survey of Pol. Ec.*, 1871), "political economy is known almost to the bottom; almost all purely economical questions may be solved, and the greater part of future discussions consists of drawing deductions from the fundamental properties of capital. Its momentousness must, in the first place, be impressed upon the mind of every student of political economy. Man without capital is as purely a fiction of the imagination as a line without breadth or a point without magnitude. It is as essential to the continuance of life as air. It is the breath of industry."

If the term capital conveys no definite meaning, of what a jargon must nearly all the problems and theorems of the so-called science consist! In Mill's own words, "A branch may be diseased and all the rest healthy; but unsoundness at the root diffuses unhealthiness through the whole tree." And it is in speaking of this very idea of capital that this apt illustration is called forth. Consequently it behoves us to ascertain, first, whether the term really has one clear meaning, and secondly, whether it is used in the same sense by those whose works on the subject are studied. And, in order to answer these questions, let us begin by laying side by side two or three definitions of capital extracted from well-known works.

In the *Principles of Political Economy*, by J. S. Mill, 1865, we find the following not very concise definition:—"What capital does for production is to afford the shelter, protection, tools, and materials which the work requires, and to feed and otherwise maintain the labourers during the process. Whatever things are destined for this use—destined to supply productive labour with these various prerequisites—are capital."

In the *Manual of Political Economy*, by Professor H. Fawcett, 1865, the following is the definition given:—"The wealth which has been accumulated with the object of assisting production is termed capital; and therefore the capital of the country is the wealth which is not immediately consumed unproductively, and which may, consequently, be devoted to assist the further production of wealth." We are not aware that this statement has been materially altered in later editions.

In a work entitled, *Political Economy for Plain People*, by Mr. G. P. Scrope, 1873, it is written— "We should therefore define capital as *that portion of movable stock which is employed or reserved for employ-*

*ment in production;* to which we would add (in order to avoid ambiguity as far as possible) *with a view to profit by the sale of its produce."*

Mill's definition may be translated into a single proposition thus:—" Whatever things are destined to supply productive labour with the shelter, protection, tools, and materials which the work requires, and to feed and otherwise maintain the labourers during the process, are capital." Mr. Scrope's definition already fulfils this desideratum, if the italics, which are his own, be read separately. But Professor Fawcett's definition, though, to use his own words, "it is a wide definition," will be found on closer inspection to be two wide definitions, of which the second embraces some things and excludes others not embraced and excluded by the first, although they are connected by the form used to indicate identical propositions. According to the first the intention of the accumulator constitutes an essential factor in the conception. In the second the possible destiny of the wealth takes the place of the accumulator's intention. There is much wealth which, though not accumulated with the *object* of assisting production, nevertheless *may* be devoted to that purpose. Such wealth is capital according to the second definition, but *not* capital according to the first. If Professor Fawcett had devoted more time to the study of logic and less to the study of mathematics, at which he looks back with so much satisfaction, he might have avoided a *non sequitur* like this. No doubt he was led to it by the laudable desire to eliminate from the conception of capital that element of destiny which is so prominent in the definition of the great logician. We are enabled, he no doubt said to himself, with this clue, to look back and declare pretty accurately what *was* capital so many years ago, and in so many years to come we shall be similarly able to decide what is capital to-day; but by what conceivable process can we point among the things around us which are capital and which are not if that depends entirely on their destiny? The eventual destiny of a thing is not necessarily coincident with the present intention of its possessor or of any one else; but as the latter is ascertainable and the former is not, it shall be taken as the true test of capital. And then, perchance, after coming to this determination there arose before the professor a vision of an old nobleman on the verge of the tomb, feeding his hunters on the oats that should make good porridge for his labourers, with a thrifty son and heir looking on and biding his time; and the object of the accumulator seemed a too-nice distinction between capital and not-capital; and so was superimposed the second not exactly complementary but rather optional mark. Now since it is quite possible and easy to say whether a given article may or may not by possibility be devoted to production, we have by means of these optional definitions really eliminated the metaphysical factor of destiny or fatality from the conception. And this is, we admit, very satisfactory; when lo! here comes Mr. Scrope and spoils the whole design, bringing back destiny in disguise. Disgusted with the professor's canny trick of producing one or other of his two definitions from his pocket as suits his convenience, under pretence that they are equivalent, Mr. Scrope rolls the two into one. Instead of this class *or* that class, he says both this class *and* that class are capital; both those things which are *reserved* for employment in production, and also those things which, whether so reserved or not, actually are so employed. It is almost a pity he did not substitute " may by possibility be employed" for " are employed." We should so have bid farewell for ever to destiny. But alas! what means that which *is* employed? Of what *particular* thing can we say that it *is* employed in production? Certainly not of any kind of so-called circulating capital. Here is a sack of oats. It certainly has not been employed in production or it would not be oats, and as to whether it will be so employed or not it is impossible to predict with certainty: after all, it is again a question of destiny.

So that, on the one hand, the wealth which, though intended for the purchase of luxury, is eventually rescued from destruction by some accident, such as the death of its possessor; and, on the other hand, that which, though intended to assist the further production of wealth, stands an equal chance of being wasted; are both included under the head of capital. Heads I win, tails you lose: in either case Mr. Scrope smiles on the wealth around him and dubs it capital.

Concerning this factor, intention, M. Courcelle Seneuil writes (*Traité d'Economie Politique*, 1867, page 49)—"Comme notre définition du mot *capital* diffère de celle qui est généralement admise, et qui a été accréditée par les auteurs les plus respectables, il est nécessaire de donner à ce sujet une courte explication. La plupart des économistes comprennent sous le nom commun de capital cette parti seulement des richesses existantes que ses possesseurs ont *l'intention* de conserver ou de reproduire par l'industrie. Ainsi tel objet compté entre les richesses serait ou ne serait pas capital selon l'intention de son possesseur, et acquerrait ou perdrait la qualité de capital selon les changements que subirait cette intention. Une telle classification a le défaut de ne s'attacher à aucun fait matériel sensible; le même objet deviendrait ou cesserait d'être capital en changeant de proprietaire: un pain, par exemple, serait capital dans la boutique du boulanger, mais une fois acquis par le consommateur, il ne serait plus un capital. Qui ne voit tout ce qu'une telle classification a de conventionnel et d'arbitraire? Mieux vaut ramener le mot capital à son acception vulgaire, d'après laquelle il désigne une somme de richesses, d'utilités existantes crées par un travail antérieur."

This popular definition is almost identical with the one adopted by J. B. Say, though it is only fair to the latter to add that he distinguished between *capital productif* and *capital improductif*, denoting by the first what is commonly denominated capital by the English economists—namely, in Bastiat's rough categories, "tools, materials, provisions." Though heartily admitting the force of M. Courcelle Seneuil's critical arguments against the current acceptation of the term, we cannot find that he makes any use, in his two cumbrous and erudite volumes, of the popular conception. We concur rather with Mr. Macdonnel in regretting that a useful term should be wasted. "J. B. Say seems to have needlessly spoiled a term which fitted a well-defined idea," or rather, we should say, a very vague idea, which, however, deserves to be well-defined.

McCulloch's definition agrees with what we must call Professor Fawcett's second definition—"The capital of a country consists of those portions of the produce of industry existing in it which are DIRECTLY available either for the support of human beings or the facilitating of production." When Mr. Macdonnel says that "whatever wealth, labour excluded, is devoted to help to form new wealth is capital," we must interpret "devoted" in the sense of "already applied" or of "intended to be applied" to the said purpose, to either of which senses our objections apply.

On the whole, then, after comparison, we give the preference to Mill's definition. And no doubt it is the most representative of the generally-accepted usage of the term. So for the purposes of this article we shall mainly confine ourselves to the condensed form of it given above—namely, "Whatever things are destined to supply productive labour with the shelter, protection, tools, and materials which the work requires, and to feed and otherwise maintain the labourers during the process, are capital."

Now, passing over the objectionable factor destiny, and assuming for the present that the destination of an article may be approximately coincident with the present intention of its possessor, even then the definition is merely one of enumeration. What is a quadruped? A quadruped is a horse, or a rat, or an elephant, or a pig, or—&c., without any reference to the distinctive attributes of the class. Of what conceivable use is such a definition? You may walk through a forest, and every now and then mark a tree with chalk. When you have done, no doubt a certain class does exist—viz., the chalked trees. But, so far as scientific utility is concerned, the classification might just as well never have been made. If the enumeration be exhaustive we may have a very distinct idea of the various things *denoted* by capital; but what we want is an equally distinct idea of the attributes *connoted* by the term.

Until we have found the connotation of a term it cannot be said to have been defined, though it may have been translated into other words.

But the connotation of a term is often implied before it is expressed, because it is often felt before it is seen. Even in the case of the chalked trees the grouping may be of use provided you were guided in your selection by some clearly or dimly recognised features common to all the trees chalked and peculiar to them. And so it is with capital. That there is an actual something approximately common and peculiar to all the groups of things enumerated in Mill's definition of capital we do not deny. On the contrary, we believe that it is this vaguely-conceived connotation which has enabled economists to do so much work with the classification; just as a chemist may do good work with an ill-understood or impure chemical. And it is this something which we intend to-day to bring into the light of day shorn of its imperfections and denuded of the fog which has hitherto surrounded it. Like tainted water in the kitchen, it has been mixed with all our food, doing more harm in some quarters than in others, and, on the whole, sufficing better than no water at all. What classes have suffered most from the pollution we shall point out on a future occasion.

The best recipe for exposing the weakness of a so-called definition by enumeration is to hunt it down through all the groups said to be comprised within it, and, by selecting extreme examples of each, to show how they are at variance with the vaguely-implied connotation as interpreted by common sense. This we will now proceed to do. First case. Here is a cotton mill, with machinery, coal, cotton, oil, an organised body of workpeople, and every other evidence of being devoted to production. It is burnt down. Was it capital? Common sense, guided by a vague perception of the connotation of the term, answers, It was capital: but the definition says, No; it was not destined to assist production, and therefore it was not capital.

Second example. A Scotch nobleman has a hundred sacks of oats, intended to be consumed by his hunters: he dies, and his thrifty heir converts the oats into porridge for his workpeople. Were the oats capital? Mill says Yes, and common sense thinks so too, while Professor Fawcett first says No, and then says Yes.

Third example. A thousand colliers on the eve of a monster meeting eat their suppers, not knowing whether a strike will commence on the morrow or not. Is their supper capital? Mill gives it up; so does Mr. Scrope; and so does Professor Fawcett, till, on second thoughts, he says. it may possibly be devoted to production, and therefore it is capital. Common sense feels that it is capital.

Quitting destiny, the next factor that merits attention is productive labour. The commodity in question may be destined to supply labour with the shelter, protection, tools, or materials which the work requires, but unless that labour be *productive* labour the article is not capital. And now arises the question, What is productive labour? Half-a-dozen different answers are at once forthcoming. M. Say confers that title upon all labour which results in utilities, or, in other words, gives pleasure to others. Mr. McCulloch goes one step further, and includes all labour which gives pleasure even to the labourer, such as eating turtle or blowing bubbles; Mr. Mill rejects all utilities that are not capable of being embodied mediately or immediately in material objects other than human, while the stricter sect exclude all that cannot at once be carried off: for example, Mill regards as productive labour the work of the schoolmaster, because eventually the country will be the richer for it materially; but not until the country is the richer for it will Professors Scrope and Fawcett pay any regard to it; and even then, if it comes through the medium of the skill of labourers, as it needs must, the former refuses to class the new increment as due to capital, but rather as due to labour. We will, however, as heretofore, follow Mill. According to him, productive labour includes "only those kinds of exertion which produce utilities embodied in material objects" as the direct or the ultimate result. Lest we should appear to some wilfully to misunderstand Mill's exact meaning, and to complicate purposely this definition within a definition, we shall do well to quote him on this point in full. "I shall . . . understand . . . by productive labour only those kinds of exertion which produce utilities embodied in material objects. But in limiting myself to this sense of the word I mean to avail myself of the full extent of that restricted acceptation, and I shall not refuse the appellation productive to labour which yields no material product as its direct result, provided that an increase of material products is its ultimate consequence." As examples of this indirectly or mediately productive labour, he cites the labour expended in the acquisition of manufacturing skill, and the labour of officers of government in affording the protection which is indispensable to the prosperity of industry.

Now the only objection we have to offer to this definition is, that it can have no conceivable application. It is clearly impossible to draw a line—even a rough line—between labour that will eventually conduce to material wealth and labour that will not. We have already admitted the labour of the educator and the government officer, and it will be hard to exclude the soldier and the tragedian, if one will but think of the ultimate effects of their work. To avoid the indefinite extension of the class Mill had recourse to a new boundary line; he again falls back on the intention of the labourer or worker. Concerning the labour of the musical performer, actor, and showman, he observes—"Some good may, no doubt, be produced, beyond the moment, upon the feelings and disposition or general state of enjoyment of the spectators; or, instead of good, there may be harm; but neither the one nor the other is the effect intended, is the result for which the exhibitor works and the spectator pays: nothing but the immediate pleasure." Surely this sudden change of front is lamentable—is inadmissible. We follow tediously the consequences of a given action through several generations down to the final embodiment of its resulting utility in a material object, and we triumphantly claim for the said action the title of productive labour, when to our chagrin we are met by the very prescriber of the requisite qualification with the objection that such embodiment was not the original object of the worker. May we not safely retort that such is not the aim of anything like half the labourers whose work has been styled productive —of the soldier, for instance, or the clergyman? Nor should we better ourselves by accepting any other economist's definition of productive labour in preference to Mill's.

We must, therefore, take things as we find them, and having obtained the value of productive labour in known terms, we will substitute them in the original equation; and we have the following:—" Whatever things are destined to supply those kinds of exertion which produce utilities immediately or mediately embodied in material objects, with the shelter, &c., &c., are capital."

And now, in order to apply that designation to any given article, we have to ascertain not only what it is destined to be devoted to, but also whether the utility possibly resulting from it is ever destined to be embodied in material objects; and further whether, if so, such embodiment was the intention of its original employer.

We are still on the threshold of our inquiry. We now arrive at the consideration of the separate groups of things which alone, even under the above-mentioned circumstances, can be classed as capital. And the first of these is shelter. It will be remembered that Mr. Scrope is careful to reject everything as capital which is not movable. But shelter is usually afforded by something immovable, such as a roof and walls. The warehouse that protects the finished goods is to be rejected; the light shed that protects the machinery is also to be rejected. The tarpaulin that protects the waggons in the yard is or is not included according to the nature of the fastenings by which it is connected with the poles in the earth: while the umbrella, beneath whose grateful shelter the foreman inspects the works and the workers, is unmistakably capital of the first water, being very movable.

Surely political economy had its origin long prior to the days of Adam Smith in the brains of the ancient lawyers, who distinguished real from personal property on the grounds that no man, be he ever so feloniously disposed, can run away with an acre of land. We lay stress on this movable qualification, because, though not expressly contained in Mill's definition, it is throughout his work assumed to be so contained, and everywhere land and its appurtenances are excluded from the category of capital.

The next station at which we shall stop is "protection." Does this include the high wall that wards off the thief; the iron bars in front of the jeweller's window; the policeman who watches the premises; the law that protects the property of citizens? All, any, or none of these? Mill's definition would, we suppose, include all; but in practice, as we have said, he excludes all things attached to the soil. Professors Fawcett and Scrope would exclude also the policeman and the law, except in so far as the latter is embodied in material statute-books, more or less movable. Let not the reader smile at these divisions and differences. Even the silliest of them has its origin in philosophical distinctions more or less profound.

Nor does the term "tools" convey any clearer meaning. Is the anvil a tool as well as the hammer?

the chimney as well as the bellows? the stream as well as the waterwheel? the steam as well as the piston? the coal as well as the boiler? It would be hard to draw the line between them: yet would any of the above-named economists call the wind that fills the sail capital? And similarly with materials. We do not seem to emerge from the fog as we advance. What, in the name of clear conception, are materials? There is a branch of them known as raw materials. Here is a piece of undyed cloth. It is the dyer's raw material, and therefore, by definition, capital. Again, here is a plastered house, destined to be painted custard-colour, according to the genius of the English people. Evidently it is precisely in the situation of the undyed cloth; and therefore it must be regarded as the painter's capital. Is it so regarded? Everything, in short, destined to be improved, repaired, touched up, is capital; and hence the greater the quantity of unfinished articles in a country, the greater its potential capital. So that we may create capital by scratching the paint off a neighbour's door, because the door will probably soon become raw material in the hands of the painter. The fog thickens.

We need not push materials any further; but after noting that the shelter, protection, tools, and materials must not only be devoted to, but actually required by, the work in order to merit the title of capital, we will proceed to consider the next group of commodities included under Mill's definition. Whatever things are destined to feed and otherwise maintain the labourers during the process are also capital. Further on Mill admits that not all the food, but only so much as is absolutely requisite to enable the labourers to perform their share of the work, is capital. Now unless we are prepared to show how much of John's beer, bread, and beef goes to the repair of John's muscles and motor nerves, and to what extent the latter are actually confined to the work he has to do, we cannot perceive of what use the term capital can be to science. How can we compare profits with capital quantitatively—that is, find the ratio of profits to capital—unless we can measure both? Again, one bootmaker, devouring in one week fifty shillings' worth of turtle, venison, and old port, works hard and turns out six pairs of boots; are the sources of his strength to be deemed all capital? It may be that a smaller quantity of the same stuff would not have sufficed to have supported him, any more than a reduction could have been made in the amount of beer, beef, and bread consumed by another bootmaker at a cost of fifteen shillings, who turns out an equal number of similar boots. There is no stipulation in the definition as to the kind of food that may be called capital; but only that the quantity must not exceed that which is actually converted into labour.*

---

\* Mr. Macdonnel handles this question in rather a remarkable and amusing manner. After putting the question whether a bottle of champagne is or is not capital, he answers that it depends upon circumstances. If consumed by one who produces nothing valuable it is not capital (but *was* it?). If by

As to those things which otherwise maintain the labourers, no doubt clothes, fuel, and shelter are meant, but so dense is the mist already surrounding us, that even this cloud adds little or nothing to the darkness.

And so, having at last groped our way to the end of our journey, we confess with disappointment that the currently-accepted and best definition of capital, apparently clear and definite enough when seen at a distance, on nearer and closer scrutiny " dissolves, and, like the baseless fabric of th' air vision, leaves not a rack behind."

Enough of this sort of analysis is as good as a feast. In fact, some people have no sympathy with us in such work; and, indeed, get very angry when we attempt it.

"In political economy," says Mr. Scrope, " much labour has been expended in vain, and great confusion introduced, where all is really plain enough, by over-*refining* and by ill-judged endeavours to give a mathe-

---

one who produces something valuable, then it is capital; " or, to be accurate, so much of the value of it as would have bought equal nourishment forms capital, the rest being purely unproductive expenditure."

So that not the champagne, or even part of it, which would not have sufficed to afford the requisite stimulus, but part of the value of the whole of the champagne, is capital. The value, not the matter, is capital. This recalls the definition of J. B. Say—" Le valeur de toutes ces choses" (before enumerated) " compose ce qu'on appelle un capital productif."

Laughable as this shuffle appears, it is paralleled, and indeed eclipsed, by the feats of legerdemain performed by Mill himself and his whole army of disciples, which we have yet to expose.

matical accuracy to definitions and propositions, which, from the nature of their subject, can pretend to no more than the grouping of phenomena according to their most striking general characters." But what are the most striking general characters of those things which are grouped together under the head of capital? That is precisely what we want to get at—the connotation of the term.

However, let us lay aside our dissecting-knife, and assume that, to all practical intents and purposes, our political economists mean roughly to comprise in the class just what Bastiat groups together as "tools, materials, provisions," and that the variance between them is due to a desire to be more exact; one regarding this feature, another that, as most requiring elucidation or qualification; let us grant that all these various and elaborate definitions do but testify to a consciousness of the imperfection of the original proposition, embodied in so many qualifying clauses. Be it so. Tools, materials, provisions; this is what is meant in plain words by capital. We will ask no questions about anvils and chimneys; we will ask no questions about raw materials and painted houses; we will ask no questions about venison and beef, beer and port wine. After all, honest folks know what they are talking about when they speak of tools, of materials, and of provisions. Like good children, we will not ask troublesome questions.

Now may we not say we know what capital is—at least roughly? Not a bit of it. Just as we begin to try and accommodate ourselves to loose forms of speech and to rest content with tolerably clear ideas of things, all our limits are suddenly swept away by the intrusion of two new elements into the conception, both wholly subversive of our newly-found interpretation of the term.

In two extraordinary propositions we are informed, firstly, that anything of value whatsoever, which can be exchanged for capital as defined, is itself capital; by which we must understand anything of value whatsoever, for the value of a thing means that it can be exchanged for other things; secondly, that there is no such thing at all as capital in an absolute sense, but that an article may be *capital* in relation to one person, *not capital* in relation to another person.

These statements seem so remarkable that they must be borne out by suitable quotations from the works of our representative economist, Mill. Speaking of a man's capital on page 69 of the *Principles*, he says, " What, then, is his capital? Precisely that part of his possessions which is to constitute his fund for carrying on fresh production. It is of no consequence that a part or even the whole of it is in a form in which it cannot directly supply the wants of the labourers." Again, in page 71, " Whether all these values are in a shape directly applicable to productive uses makes no difference. Their shape, whatever it may be, is a temporary accident; but once destined for production, they do not fail to find a way of transforming themselves into things capable of being applied to it."

To some minds it would appear almost desirable to

employ two technical terms—one to designate the group of articles hitherto classed together as capital, and another to designate whatever of value is destined to be exchanged for such capital. But as in our opinion both terms would be of no conceivable use to exact science, we shall not waste space in converting one bad tool into two not much better. Let us rather prepare ourselves for the second revelation, to the effect that, after all, there is no such thing as capital *per se*. Speaking of a particular instance, Mill, on page 74 of the *Principles*, writes—" In the present instance that which is virtually capital to the individual is or is not capital to the nation according as the fund which, by the supposition he has not dissipated, has or has not been dissipated by somebody else." In other words, wealth which is capital to an individual may be not capital to the nation or another individual or group of individuals. The same article is capital to A, not capital to B; and capital is, therefore, merely a relative term—*i.e.*, implies a particular relation between a particular person and a particular thing.

Our original definition, to be more accurate, requires to be so expanded as to embody these two new important factors somehow or other. We submit the following :—

" Whatever things are destined to supply those kinds of exertion which produce utilities immediately or mediately embodied (and originally intended to be embodied) in material objects with the shelter, protection, tools, and materials which the work requires; and to feed and otherwise maintain the labourers during the process; or whatever things are capable of being and destined to be exchanged for such, are, in relation to some person or persons, according to circumstances not specified, capital." Or, to adopt Bastiat's abbreviated form, as we have consented to do, "Tools, materials, provisions, and whatsoever is intended or destined to be exchanged for such, are capital with respect to somebody."

Our determination to look at things kindly, and, as Mr. Scrope advises us, with our eyes half-closed, has, we fear, landed us in a quagmire not much superior to that in which our method of analysis terminated.

If we really wish to know what the term capital means we *must* have recourse to the comparative method; and by extracting that which is common and peculiar to all forms of so-called capital that we can bring together within our field of vision, finally discover the true connotation, instead of barely enumerating the more convenient forms, and averting our gaze from the ugly borderland specimens, the ornithorhynchuses and pterodactyluses of our kingdom.

Let us commence operations by colligating the following cases drawn together from various points of the compass:—

The above-mentioned factory in working order before it is burnt down.

The hundred sacks of oats intended for his hunters by the above-mentioned old nobleman.

The slaves on a sugar-plantation.

The tall chimney which causes the strong draught in a boiler-house.

An acre of plough land in Middlesex.

An acre of land on the banks of Lake Tanyanyika.

A casket of diamonds cut and polished.

We shall assume that common sense, or rather the opinion of all those whose vague idea of capital is sufficiently clear to cause them to desire a term or name for the conception, will admit that of this group of cases the first five are capital and the last two not capital. What we have to do is to find out what is common to the five and not common to the last two.

And, first of all, we see that the element of destiny is excluded by the factory, which by supposition is not destined to produce new wealth. Next we see that the intention of the possessor does not affect the question, for although the oats are intended to be unproductively consumed, yet they are regarded as capital.

The case of the slaves disposes of the allegation that man is not capital, "but only that for which capital exists."

The tall chimney excludes the factor movability, which, but for high authorities, we should hardly have considered worthy of express exclusion.

And land may or may not be capital according to

circumstances, for in Middlesex we regard it as such, but not on the banks of Tanyanyika.

Lastly, value is not a sufficient mark, for the diamonds are not capital, though no one will dispute their value.

Up to the present we can only see two factors common to the five examples of capital. Firstly, they all possess value; and, secondly, they are all originally fit or suitable for the production of wealth. They contain a possibility of helping to form new capital.

But value is already excluded because it is not only common to the forms of capital, but also to the casket of diamonds. Nor are we more fortunate with our potentiality; for there is that in the acre of land on the shores of the African lake which would enable it to assist in the production of new wealth—viz., a fertile soil. Moreover, the wind that turns the mill-sails and drives the ship contributes most unmistakably to the creation of wealth, and yet it is not capital.

To what straits, then, are we driven!

It seems as though there were no attribute at once common to all forms of wealth properly called capital, and yet peculiar to them. Nor does any amount of search and scrutiny serve to throw any light on the position. If we increase the number of cases we are no better off. Have we not tried everything, and in vain? Must we, after all, give it up? One more attempt. Value is common to all, and fitness to assist in the creation of new wealth is also common to all. Yet neither of these attributes is peculiar to capital.

o

May it be that the combination of the two is the required connotation? We feel we are getting nearer. The wind that helps to create wealth has no value, and the diamonds that have great value help to create no wealth. Alas! consider these bananas at Covent Garden. They are sold for threepence each, and are therefore very valuable. Humboldt calculated the productiveness as compared with that of wheat as 133 to 1; and in many parts of India and the West Indies they form the chief food of labourers. Yet as we look at them we feel they are not capital. Again, this fibrous variety of actinolite, called asbestos from its incombustibility, has been utilised, and would be in a hundred ways in the shape of incombustible cloth (for its fibres are as fine as flax) but for its high value.

But though disappointed we can no longer be withstood. The truth flashes in upon us. The connotation of capital rends its veil of mist and gloom and comes forth clear, sharply-defined, and brilliant as a crystal. Once seen there is no mistaking it.

"Capital is that the value of which is *due* to the value of its products."

It is not long, it is not vague, but pithy, transparent, and to the point. Anything which owes its value to the demand, not for itself, as calculated to afford immediate gratification to the consumer, but for some other commodity into the creation of which it enters as an element, whether as raw material, as tool or machine, as worker, brute or human—such a thing is capital.

If the value of a commodity partly consumed for its own sake, partly in the manufacture of other articles (as coals, for example), varies with the value of the goods manufactured by means of it, it is clearly capital; whether or no the portion of it under consideration be or be not destined for immediate consumption.

With this key we at once and easily unlock all difficulties. Take the piece of undyed cloth. Is it capital in the hands of the dyer? In order to answer this question, we first inquire whether the value of the said cloth is due to the demand for it in the dyed state. If so, if the immediate consumer does not offer so high a price for the undyed material as the dyer can afford to do, then it is capital. Take the diamonds, supposing them to be of a fair size. Are they capital? Clearly the polisher or glass-cutter cannot afford to buy them for the purposes of his trade at the value their unassisted pleasure-giving power can command in the market as ornaments; hence they are not capital.

Is venison capital? Certainly not. Because its value is due, not to the demand for the products into which it may enter (as labourers, for instance), but to its intrinsic power of affording immediate gratification.

Is bread capital in England? In order to answer this question we must ascertain whether an extended demand for any commodity into which bread enters as an element causes a rise in the value of bread. Unquestionably an extended demand for labourers (or, as is commonly said, for labour) is followed by a rise in the value of bread, other things equal. Hence bread is capital in England. And so on with any commodity that may be proposed for consideration.

Having found the key and tested its powers we might stop here, leaving the definition to its fate in the sure knowledge that it will be accepted by all succeeding political economists. Indeed, it only requires to be stated in order to be received.

But, like all other important innovations, our new definition cuts away so much rubbish and lumber that we feel bound to clear away some of the *débris*, and to see our vessel fairly launched before quitting it.

In the first place, both land and labourers must be reinstated under the head of capital; for clearly the value of labourers is entirely due to the value of their productions, and not to the gratification obtainable from them immediately, except in a few cases, such as singers, dancers, parsons, and the like, who in the exercise of their functions cause direct satisfaction.

Labourers in general, commonly so called—that is to say, human beings engaged in the creation of new forms of valuable *matter*, whether by manual exertion or as managers, superintendents, co-ordinators, or inventors—are capital. There is nothing new in this. It has been admitted, for various insufficient reasons, by some of our shrewdest economists.

McCulloch (*Principles*, page 116) writes—" However extended the sense previously attached to the term capital may at first sight appear, we are inclined to think that it should be interpreted still more comprehensively. Instead of understanding by capital all that portion of the produce of industry *extrinsic* to man which may be made applicable to his support and to the facilitating of production, there does not seem to be any good reason why man himself should not, and very many why he should, be considered as forming a part of the national capital. Man is as much the produce of previous outlays of wealth expended on his subsistence, education, &c., as any of the instruments constructed by his agency; and it would seem that in those inquiries which regard only his mechanical operations, and do not involve the consideration of his higher and nobler powers, he should be regarded in precisely the same point of view. Every individual who has arrived at maturity, though he may not be instructed in any particular art or profession, may yet, with perfect propriety, be viewed in relation to his natural powers as a machine which it has cost twenty years of assiduous attention and the expenditure of a considerable capital to construct. And if a further sum be expended in qualifying him for the exercise of a business or profession requiring unusual skill, his value will be proportionally increased, and he will be entitled to a greater reward for his exertions, as a machine becomes more valuable when it acquires new powers by the expenditure of additional capital or labour in its construction. Adam Smith has fully admitted the justice of this principle, though he has not reasoned consistently from it. He states that the acquired and useful talents of the inhabitants should be considered as forming a portion of the national capital. 'The acquisition of such talents,' he justly observes, 'during the education, study, or apprenticeship of the acquirer always costs a real expense, which is a capital fixed and realised, as it were, in his person.'"

Unfortunately McCulloch finds himself just as unable to cope with his new principle as Smith did before him, not because it was a false one, but because it was based by both on a false reasoning, a rotten foundation.

Nor is it by any means new to comprehend land under the head of capital, though we are in a minority in so doing. Mr. Macdonnel passes this criticism on the English economists, after comprising land under materials or tools, and therefore under capital:—
"This is, indeed, contrary to the usage of English economists, who put land, the representative of all other natural agents, in a category by itself. But two reasons, I think, warrant a deviation. In the first place the classification of English economists with regard to this point involves an inconsistency; for though laying it down—to take Mr. Fawcett as their spokesman—'that capital is all that wealth, in whatever shape or form it may exist, which is set aside to assist future production,' and though of course viewing land as a portion of wealth, they exclude land from the kinds of wealth included under capital."

However, without troubling ourselves to examine authorities on this point further, we perceive that under capital fall both land and labourers—not labour, which is a mere metaphysical entity, or, what comes to the same thing, no entity at all; but labourers.

Strange to say, this confusion of materials with forces is made by all the leading economists without exception, including even the great logician and philosopher, J. S. Mill, who says—" The human being himself I do not class as wealth. He is the purpose for which wealth exists." And then he proceeds to class his ability to work under the head of labour. " But his acquired capacities, which exist only as means, and have been called into existence by labour, fall rightly, as it seems to me, within that designation."

A weak objection to classing labour under the head of capital is offered by Mr. Scrope in the form of a criticism on Mr. McCulloch's opinion, just quoted.

"We need hardly observe," he says, " that things which are identical can have no reciprocal action on each other:" from which we are to conclude that if land and labour be capital, disquisitions on the reciprocal influence of land, labour, and other kinds of capital; of rent, wages, and other kinds of profit, must needs be vain delusions and absurdities. We would remind Mr. Scrope that species of one genus may differ considerably amongst themselves, and may act and react one upon another to any extent, notwithstanding the fact that they have attributes in common.

Nor is it disputed that there are well-marked species or sub-classes of capital which are approximately coincident with the old so-styled genera, land and labourers: and it is this fact which gives value to the problems and theorems contained in works which are based upon an erroneous view of the term capital. Were it not so the whole tree would indeed be rotten because of the disease at the root.

But no one denies that, of all kinds of capital, human beings alone have this peculiarity, that they are the cause of values as well as the part-cause of valuables. No wonder labourers are a very marked and distinct sub-class of capital!

Land, too, has most important peculiarities, into which we will not enter here. Rarities are often classed together and distinguished by a class mark. For instance, we talk of monopoly prices in speaking of coal, of the works of the old masters, and the like. Then there is the well-known division of capital into fixed and circulating, which we will now proceed briefly to consider: and at the same time we must point out that this division testifies to a real but vaguely-discerned distinction which underlies the flimsy one commonly alleged. We are told (Mill's *Principles*, p. 114), "Of the capital engaged in the production of any commodity there is a part which, after being once used, exists no longer as capital; is no longer capable of rendering service to production, or at least not the same service, nor to the same sort of production. . . . Capital which in this manner fulfils the whole of its office in the production in which it is engaged, by a single use, is called circulating capital. . . . Another large portion of capital, however, consists in instruments of production of a more or less permanent character; which produce their effect, not by being parted with, but by being kept; and the efficacy of which is not exhausted by a single use. . . . Capital which exists in any of these durable shapes, and the return to which is spread over a period of corresponding duration, is called fixed capital."

So that the distinction appears to consist in the number of times a given commodity may be employed in the same process; those which can be employed only once being called circulating; those which can be employed more than once, fixed.

Now to us it seems that, although in ninety-nine cases out of a hundred fixed capital suffices for more than one process, and circulating capital for only one, yet these are but accidental and not the essential characteristics of the two classes.

The real distinction lies deeper. It is this: those things the eventual consumption of which is essential to the creation of the required compound or new product form one class, vaguely indicated by the term *circulating*: those things the eventual consumption of which is not essential, but only accidental, to the creation of the required compound, form another class—*fixed* capital. No doubt all capital is consumed, but so is everything else; the iron ladle required to stir this molten metal soon wears out and must be renewed. If it wore out in one use, as the wick of a candle is destroyed as fast as the tallow, Mill would call it circulating capital. So with a quill pen. One day's use destroys it.

Yet we maintain that the ladle, the wick, and the pen are all (so far as they are capital at all) fixed capital. Why? Because, if they never wore out at all, even after a million processes, so far from being less useful, they would not only not impair the product to which they contribute, but rather render it more pure. The gold pen with which this is written has been in use for five years, and is in no wise worse than when it was new. And so with a permanent wick in an oil-lamp: but not so with the oil or tallow. If that were not changed, consumed, the lamp or candle would give no light, the sempstress would not see to work, and the produce, shirt or dress, would not be made.

The number of processes for which an article will serve is quite immaterial to science; it is a mere question of degree of durability, and we can base upon it no such valuable philosophical classification as can be based upon the distinction between essentially and only accidentally consumed capital. And here we may point out that this very distinction is the one which underlies the division of capital into *tools* and *materials*. Tools are exactly what we have defined as fixed or accidentally consumed capital. Materials are our circulating or essentially consumed capital. This discovery of identity, and the conception upon which the classes have hitherto been instinctively based, are of immense importance in the study of plutology.

And now, in conclusion, we may here state, and, with the aid of our new light, with advantage scrutinise, Mill's four theorems concerning capital.

The first is that industry is limited by capital. Now if this means that the creation of new wealth is limited by the quantity of the materials which enter into its constitution, the so-called theorem is merely a truism. But if it mean that it is limited by the quantity of capital *other than human* (which it evidently must do consistently with Mill's doctrines), it amounts to saying generally that where one of the elements is wanting the compound containing it cannot be produced: also a truism. However, it so happens that there are such compounds as combinations of labourers and not capital; as, for example, a stone statue. Sculpture, provided the material used be not valuable, is an industry not limited by any capital other than labourers. According to Mill's own notion of capital, therefore, his first theorem is false.

The second theorem is that capital is the result of saving. Now in what conceivable sense can it be said of a new and useful invention that it is the result of saving? And yet it may be, and usually is, capital in the highest degree. Or how is a newly-found oil-well the result of saving? And yet it is unquestionably capital. No doubt, in so far as articles capable of affording immediate gratification are by preference combined with others for the purpose of producing more valuable products, these products are the result of saving; and it is also true that most products do contain such saved elements. But we do not want half-truths or accidental truths to stand for general or necessary truths; and, so judged, the second theorem is false.

The third theorem is that capital is consumed. This proposition we have already discussed in treating of the division into fixed and circulating capital.

We have shown that it is not of the essence of fixed capital to be consumed. All things are ever changing, of course. But it is no more essential to fixed capital to wear out than it is to a silver teapot to contain a small quantity of lead, indisputable though the fact may be as a merely accidental fact.

So that here we have a universal but accidental proposition standing for an essential truth.

The fourth theorem is that a demand for commodities is not a demand for labour. It is difficult to translate this into scientific language, but, so far as it is intelligible, it seems to be either a truism or misleading. Consider the two following statements:—
A demand for iron ore is not a demand for limestone and coal. A demand for grapes is not a demand for apples. There is a wide difference between the two negations; for in the first case a demand for iron ore is accompanied by a demand for limestone and coal invariably, and it may roughly be said that a demand for the one is a demand for the other two. To say that it is not so is to state a truism of the

weakest order, being based simply on the literal meaning of the words. But in the case of the grapes the negation is of a different character. A demand for grapes is not accompanied by a demand for apples, which is in no wise affected thereby.

If we criticise Mill's theorem in the first sense, then we have a miserable truism to deal with. A demand for one thing is not, and cannot be, a demand for another.

But if we regard it in the second sense, and inquire whether a demand for commodities is or is not invariably accompanied by a demand for labourers, we contend that it depends, in any given case, upon the answer to the question whether the commodities demanded are or are not capital requiring the assistance of labourers in order to become capable of affording gratification. If they are such capital, then a demand for them *is* virtually a demand for labourers. If they are not such capital, then a demand for them is *not* a demand for labourers. We must condemn this theorem as being either a truism or misleading.

There cannot be stronger testimony to the harmfulness of loose thought and corresponding phraseology than is afforded by the spectacle of a great logician like Mill propounding four fundamental theorems as the basis of his work, of which it must be said that the first is false, the second is false, the third non-essential, and the fourth either a truism or misleading.

How better than by such exposition can we meet Mr. Scrope's sneer concerning the vanity of the labour which has been expended in what he calls "over-refining and ill-judged endeavours to give a mathematical accuracy to definitions and propositions which from the nature of the subject can pretend" to nothing of the sort?

With the aid of our new definition of capital and other definitions of terms at present loosely handled, we hope in future papers to build up a symmetrical, complete, and systematic science of plutology, as distinguished from the political economy still flourishing—in other words, to grope our way from the alchemy to the chemistry of values.

# WILLIAMS & NORGATE'S PUBLICATIONS.

**MIND, A QUARTERLY REVIEW OF PSYCHOLOGY AND PHILOSOPHY.** Nos. 1 and 2, Price 3s., or 12s. per Annum, Post Free.

---

### THE DOCTRINE OF EVOLUTION.

**MR. HERBERT SPENCER'S WORKS.**

**FIRST PRINCIPLES.** Third Edition. 16s.

**THE PRINCIPLES OF BIOLOGY.** 2 vols. 34s.

**THE PRINCIPLES OF PSYCHOLOGY.** 2 vols. 36s.

**THE PRINCIPLES OF SOCIOLOGY.** Vol. I. [*In the press.*

BY THE SAME AUTHOR.

**SOCIAL STATICS.** 8vo, cloth, 10s.

**EDUCATION: INTELLECTUAL, MORAL, and PHYSICAL.** 8vo, cloth, 6s.

**ESSAYS: SCIENTIFIC, POLITICAL, AND SPECULATIVE.** 2 vols. 8vo, cloth, 16s.

**ESSAYS: (Third Series) SCIENTIFIC, POLITICAL, AND SPECULATIVE.** Vol. III. Including the Classification of Sciences. 8vo, cloth, 7s. 6d.

**DESCRIPTIVE SOCIOLOGY; or, Groups of Sociological Facts, Classified and arranged by HERBERT SPENCER.** Compiled and Abstracted by DAVID DUNCAN, M.A., Professor of Logic, &c., in the Presidency College, Madras; RICHARD SCHEPPIG, Ph.D.; and JAMES COLLIER. Folio bds.

- No. 1. ENGLISH. By James Collier. 18s.
- No. 2. ANCIENT MEXICANS, CENTRAL AMERICANS, CHIBCHAS, AND ANCIENT PERUVIANS. By Dr. Scheppig. 16s.
- No. 3. TYPES OF LOWEST RACES, NEGRITTO RACES, AND MALAYO-POLYNESIAN RACES. By Professor Duncan. 18s.
- No. 4. AFRICAN RACES. By Professor Duncan. 16s.

Just published, complete in 4 parts, 25s. 6d.

A SKETCH OF A PHILOSOPHY. By JOHN MACVICAR, M.A., LL.D., D.D.

PART I.—MIND: Its Powers and Capacities. 6s.

PART II.—MATTER and MOLECULAR MORPHOLOGY. 3s. 6d.

PART III.—THE CHEMISTRY OF NATURAL SUBSTANCES. 7s.

PART IV.—BIOLOGY AND THEODICY, a Prelude to the Biology of the Future. 9s.

BARRATT (A.) PHYSICAL ETHICS, or the Science of Action: an Essay. 8vo, cloth, 12s.

FELLOWES (Robert, LL.D.) THE RELIGION OF THE UNIVERSE, with consolatory Views of a Future State. 3rd Edition. Post 8vo, cloth, 6s.

BURGESS (W. R.) THE RELATION OF LANGUAGE TO THOUGHT. Cr. 8vo, cloth, 2s. 6d.

SARGANT (W. Lucas), ESSAYS OF A BIRMINGHAM MANUFACTURER. By W. L. SARGANT, Author of "Social Innovators," "Apology for Sinking Funds," &c. 4 vols. 8vo, each 7s. 6d.

LAMING (R.) THE SPIRITUALITY OF CAUSATION, a Scientific Hypothesis. Crown 8vo, cloth, 3s.

WHAT DO WE KNOW? Eight Tracts on this Question. Leaves from the Writing-Desk of an old Student. Crown 8vo, cloth, 3s. 6d.

---

WILLIAMS AND NORGATE,
14, HENRIETTA STREET, COVENT GARDEN, LONDON;
AND 20, SOUTH FREDERICK STREET, EDINBURGH.

www.ingramcontent.com/pod-product-compliance
Lightning Source LLC
Chambersburg PA
CBHW020828230426
43666CB00007B/1142